56 Years: Two Journeys

56 Years: Two Journeys

How a Lutheran became Ignatian in his Years at
Boston College

and how Boston College stayed Ignatian as it Grew

Harold Petersen

To the Jesuits of Boston College,

Past and Present,

Who have Given us So Much

Contents

Part 3 - Resurgence and New Challenges

Part IV - Continued Growth and Stability

Acknowledgements

I am grateful to my colleagues who had the patience to read an earlier draft of this manuscript and who gave me invaluable comments, corrections, and suggestions. I note particularly the help of Ben Birnbaum, Burt Howell, David Twomey, Mary Sweeney, SC, James A. Woods, S.J., Joseph Quinn, Richard Tresch, Charles Fish, J. Joseph Burns, Joseph P. Duffy, S.J., Patricia Lowe, Jack Dunn, Thomas Sullivan, Robert Newton, Donald Petersen, and Joseph Appleyard, S.J. I didn't accede to all of their suggestions, but I did pay heed to most of them. Any remaining errors are of course my own.

I also wish to express my profound appreciation to the late J. Donald Monan, S.J., for his encouraging comments on reading parts of this work that I had written some years before, and to William P. Leahy, S.J., for his request that I produce a memoir.

The photos of Gasson Hall (front cover), of the statue of St. Ignatius and of the Football National Championship banner (back cover) are by the author. The photo of the author (back cover) is by colleague Ashley Duggan.

Preface

This is a story of one person's journey through Boston College from 1960 to 2016 and also the journey of Boston College as seen through that person's eyes. A young Lutheran came in with a fair degree of skepticism as to whether he would last at a Catholic school. He left after 56 years with a deep appreciation for the gift of Ignatian spirituality. Boston College evolved from a commuter college for first-generation college students to a cosmopolitan university of international acclaim.

What follows is offered neither as my own life story—I say very little of my family or my church or my town, all of which have been important to me—nor as a history of Boston College from 1960-2016. Rather it is a personal reflection on events in which I was directly involved or about which I heard from people who were involved. I write from memory, supplemented by what correspondence I have in my files and appointments as listed in my pocket calendars. I kept no journal at the time but the stories have stayed fresh in my memory through telling them over and over, both to students and to friends.

Memories of course can play tricks on us, so there may be errors of facts or of dates. It is my hope that I have been true to the essence of both my journey and that of the institution that has been so much a part of my life.

My own path involved learning to cope with failure and hopefully with some success. I will leave that for my students to judge. The journey of Boston College includes surviving a financial crisis in 1968-72 and a determined effort to maintain its Catholic and Jesuit identity as it grew in stature.

Boston College was decidedly a Catholic and Jesuit school in 1960 and it is so to this day. But the process of maintaining that identity, and discerning what it means to be Catholic and Jesuit with a diverse faculty that includes fewer and fewer Jesuit priests, was not an easy one.

It is my hope that what is here will be of some use to historians who might like an eyewitness account of some of the events described. It is also my hope that in reading what follows people might grasp more quickly some truths it has taken me a long time to learn. Finally, it is my hope that people might find this an enjoyable read.

Harold Petersen

Part 1 - Emergence in the Sixties

Commencement Day, 1960

My first day on the Boston College Campus was June 13, 1960. I pulled into the main gate about 10:00 a.m. and motored on down Linden Lane, having no idea it was commencement day. If it sounds a bit unlikely that I could enter without noticing unusual activity, bear in mind that those were simpler times. I parked by Gasson Hall,[i] went inside and asked someone if they knew where the economics department was. I was directed to Fulton Hall, where I found the two people from Boston College I had met, Robert J. McEwen, S.J. and Alice Bourneuf.

McEwen, who had hired me in January, was the chair of economics and Bourneuf was the person he had brought on to help him build a graduate program. I hadn't told either I would be arriving on that day, but both were most gracious. McEwen found an office for me just down the hall, or really a desk, since four of us would share an office for those first three years. He then told me he was about to go over to commencement and asked if I would like to join him. We sat high in the stands of the original alumni stadium, the one completed in 1957, listened for a bit, and then came back to Fulton. I have no idea who the commencement speaker might have been on that day or what was said in the address.

Bourneuf was there waiting for us when we got back. She invited me to come to dinner, along with McEwen, that evening at her home on Quinobequin Road. We both assented readily and I looked forward to the evening.

I then asked McEwen what might be a good place to stay while I looked for an apartment. He called a woman he knew in Newton, on Church and Waverly, who occasionally rented rooms to our graduate students. She was happy to take me, even on a short-term basis, although it turned out that her daughter was not so happy on finding that her room had been let for a pittance of cash.

I had a map of the greater Boston area and was able to locate the relevant streets. So, I went to Church and Waverly, met the kindly woman, and paid her for the first night. I picked up a newspaper, scanned the apartment listings, and then drove around a bit to acclimate myself to the area. I settled on Allston as a likely place to live but put off further search until the morrow.

While I was getting ready for dinner, my glasses broke across the bow. They were the horn-rimmed plastic frames popular at that time and the plastic had no doubt weakened over time until it was ready to break. I put a piece of tape around the break and set out. Dinner was lovely—Alice was always the most gracious host—and of course we all had a few drinks. We talked about others who would be joining the faculty and about hopes for the future.

About 9:00 p.m. I got back in my car, confident I assured both McEwen and Bourneuf, that I could find my way back. About the time I got to Beacon Street my glasses broke again and the tape, now worn, would not hold them in place. I could drive without them but could not easily read the street signs or even the small print on the map.

I missed a turn that would have taken me over to Commonwealth Avenue and then Waverly, and kept on going. By 9:30, with it now dark, I was completely lost. I found myself at the Howard Johnson's in Forest Hills and went inside to try to find out how to get back to Newton. I got lost again and found myself on Blue Hill Avenue, where I parked under a streetlight and got out with my map to see if I could find my way.

A policeman pulled up and offered to help. He no doubt saw the Ohio license plate, and the map, and took pity on me. He pointed me in the right direction and I eventually found my way back to Church and Waverly. So my first encounter with the Boston Police was highly positive. I didn't tell the officer that my driver's license stipulated glasses and he didn't ask. Nor did he ask if I had been drinking.

I must have had a guardian angel with me even then. It was an eventful first day. But I have wondered since whether the encounter on Blue Hill Avenue might have been different had I not been a White kid wearing a coat and tie. Would that same guardian angel have been there for me?

My Early Years

I grew up in a small town in northern Minnesota called Fertile. The name itself would be curious were it not such a boring story. The settlers had come from Fertile, Iowa, where the rich black soil was eight inches deep, and being sturdy folks but without a whole lot of imagination, they named their new settlement Fertile. Never mind that it was on the edge of a sand pit, the residue of Lake Agassiz as it had receded from its Southernmost shore some 10,000 years before.

On second thought, perhaps they did have some imagination, or at least a sense of humor. The town is just 20 miles north of Twin Valley and 30 miles east of Climax. Yes, Climax. That town was in fact settled fifteen years later, so it may have been those folks who really had the sense of humor. Climax was named after a brand of chewing tobacco, and that strikes me as pretty shrewd branding for a tobacco firm. Look it up if you don't believe me. We don't make this stuff up.[ii]

Could those early settlers have even imagined the jokes that would bedevil their future citizens? As when a headline appeared in *The Fertile Journal* with the greatest of innocence, "Fertile Girl Weds at Climax." Twin Valley got its name just because it was in a valley between a river and a creek. I don't know how that makes it a "twin" valley. None of the three towns have shown any population growth over the past fifty years.

Fertile is also just 24 miles south of Red Lake Falls, the county seat of Red Lake County, which was described by Christopher Ingraham in the Washington Post as "the absolute worst place to live in America." On publishing the piece in August 2015, Ingraham was asked to visit the county, which he did. On experiencing the place, he loved it so much that he moved his family there. So Red Lake Falls may be gaining population, at least for now.

Fertile was home to about 900 residents, virtually all of whom were Lutherans. Our sole doctor in town was Catholic, one of two pharmacists was Jewish, and I suppose there were a few more non-Lutherans but certainly not many. All of my grade-school classmates were Lutheran and the superintendent of the public school was also the Sunday-School superintendent at Concordia Lutheran Church. We were a little inbred.

What we were told of Catholics was that they worshiped Mary, which we Lutherans saw as idolatrous, and that they looked to the Pope as the source of authority rather than to what it said in the Bible. We trusted our doctor, even if he was Catholic, and the Jewish pharmacist was all right. What we thought of Judaism was more from the Gospel of John than from the others, and our image of Jesus was pretty much the auburn-haired, blue-eyed man who looked a lot like us except that he had a beard.

Sunday School was good for the most part. We were a gathering of friends who learned the Bible stories and were admonished to behave. That was the norm. But then about every two years we would have a visit from a travelling evangelist who would preach hell fire and damnation. We all knew we were sinners and for about three weeks following would live in mortal fear. Then we got over it, or at least most of us did.

The only Blacks I saw prior to college were the porters on the Northern Pacific, and I only saw them as they stepped off the train to put down the platform for passengers to disembark. They looked sharp in their spiffy blue jackets and sporty caps, and it struck me that they had a pretty good job. We had all listened to *Amos and Andy*[iii] on the radio, and we had read *Huckleberry Finn*, but that is about where we were in terms of race relations.

Sports were big in Fertile, and I had almost no athletic ability. When we chose up sides for basketball or softball, I would be the last kid picked. "I guess we get Petersen," is a phrase I can't quite put aside. But there were some things I was good at, including debate, theater, journalism, and academics, so life was all right. I kept trying at sports, even football until I broke a tooth against another player's helmet, but by junior year I had given up any hope of earning a letter as a member of a team.

My father was in small business, farm machinery and trucks, and I was involved in the business from the time I was about twelve. I would keep the books, send out invoices or letters, and sell parts at the counter. My dad wanted me to go into the business with him, and by junior year of high school had named the business "Jerry Petersen and Son." I wanted no part of it but didn't quite know how to tell my dad. I couldn't imagine trying to persuade a farmer to buy one of our tractors rather than that of a competitor, and I couldn't do repairs. When my dad took apart a machine he remembered exactly how to put it back together, whereas to me the scattered parts were a complete mystery.

It was my grandmother Laura's dream that I should become a Lutheran minister and I suppose about half the town expected that would be the case. After high school it would be Concordia College and then Luther Seminary in St. Paul. I was even sent to Seattle to an international convention of the Luther League in the hope that this would pull me to the ministry. I wanted no part of that either but didn't quite know how to escape. I would have been hopeless as a minister, since I couldn't carry a tune, and the pastor had to lead the singing in the Lutheran church.

Away from Fertile

I said I didn't quite know how to escape. But then a high school teacher who had attended DePauw (in Greencastle, Indiana) told me about a scholarship program that might offer up to full tuition. I applied, took an exam, and was offered a full-tuition scholarship. Dad conceded that I couldn't very well turn that down, and I was off to DePauw.

My mother was a bit concerned, as I learned much later in finding a letter from DePauw's admissions officer assuring her that there was indeed a Lutheran student association at DePauw. I joined that small band of Lutherans in a sea of Methodists and by sophomore year was president of the group.

I entered DePauw, in September 1951, with some thought of becoming a writer, and my freshman roommate was a farm kid from upstate New York who had expressed similar aspirations. That may be why they put us together. That kid from New York was John Champlin Gardner, who went on to become a leading light of American fiction until his untimely death in 1982. (Some of you may have read *Grendel* or *The Sunlight Dialogues* or *October Light*.) When I saw John's devotion to literature, and his mastery of the field even as a college freshman, it occurred to me that I should try something else. So I majored in economics.

9

John was writing a novel as a freshman and was typing well into the night. He asked me if it bothered me and I said no. Bear in mind that typewriters were not then silent, but the clicking of the keys did not keep me awake. When he finished it, he read it through and then tossed it into the wastebasket. I rescued it before the custodian came along, read parts of it and after a few weeks gave it back to him. He kept it this time and parts of it may have appeared in his later work.

John had interests in both music and writing and he was convinced he could teach anyone to sing. One evening he took me over to the music school and sat down at the piano. He played a note, vocalized it, and asked me to do so. After an hour of this nonsense, he gave it up and did not try again. I like to think I had something to do with his becoming a teacher of writing rather than of music.

John did like my freshman short story. He smiled as he read it and said, "This is the nuts." Never mind that my professor gave me a B on the paper. John's praise was much more important. For a month or two I continued to think I might be a writer. John's praise was pretty special. If you are not familiar with the phrase "This is the nuts," it is used as a superlative in Robert Penn Warren's *All the King's Men*.

DePauw was very much a fraternity-sorority school and rush was held the weekend before the start of classes. This was where people were sorted out—the Betas and the Sigma Chi's at the top and on down from there. Some of course were not accepted at all. It was understood that Blacks and Jews would not be admitted, and others who did not "fit in" were turned down by every single fraternity or sorority. This was devastating to people whose parents had counted on their becoming a Beta or at worst a Delta M.

I had received letters of interest over the summer but was ambivalent about fraternity life until I arrived at DePauw. I elected not to go through rush, as did my roommate John, and so did not experience the pain of rejection. But I did come to see how wrong the system was through the pain of others. Many of my friends who were in fraternities realized as well how damaging the system was but they cited rules of the national charter and said they were working from within to bring about change.

I joined a group called MHA (Men's Hall Association), a combination of fraternity rejects and people who wanted the positive aspects of Greek life without the exclusionary covenants. MHA welcomed anyone as a member and offered a chance to participate with the frats in intramural sports, campus governance, and social activities. MHA even had an initiation ceremony and a pin (which I have to this day). We were accepted by the "Greeks" so long as we didn't use Greek Letters in the name of our organization. It would not have been okay to call ourselves Mu Eta Alpha.

At the beginning of my junior year Vernon Jordan enrolled at DePauw. Vern was tall and handsome and articulate and black. He went through rush knowing he would be rejected, perhaps to let the brothers know what they would be missing. Vernon Jordan was extraordinarily personable and likeable. The local fraternities very much wanted him but would not risk losing their national charters.

Vern joined MHA and we became friends. He succeeded me as MHA's representative on the Student Senate (DePauw's student governing body). The members of the Senate had decided we would wear blue blazers so that the other students would know who we were and that the living units would pay for them. The guys in MHA weren't too keen about paying for my blazer just so that I could strut around with it, but they did relent and buy it for me. That meant of course that I would pass the blazer along to my successor on the Senate. Vern was a head taller than me and had longer arms. You can only imagine how that blue blazer fit.

Vernon Jordan went on to become the president of the Urban League and then a confidante of presidents. He is a loyal alumnus who even as an undergraduate gave more to DePauw than he could ever imagine.

What I gained from Vern, and from another Black student who was in my dorm, was a comfort level with Black students and a deeper awareness of what life was like for Blacks in America. I had experienced discrimination as an outlier with no ability in sports, but what these kids put up with was orders of magnitude beyond that. Vern couldn't even get a haircut in Greencastle, Indiana, even by a Black barber who didn't want to alienate his White customers.

In my sophomore year at DePauw John Gardner and I were no longer roommates but we did live in the same small dorm. John kept a journal of that year, with no idea, I am sure, that it would ever be published. I am described in there by name as a dorm councilor (an R.A.) and an instigator of pranks. (You can look that up as well. The

Journal is called *Lies! Lies! Lies!*) All I will say about that charge is that we did have a fun time and I was fortunate to retain my scholarship over the four years.

I was not a particularly serious student at DePauw, and I remember my faculty advisor chastising me for not doing better. I did enough to get by and did well enough in my math courses to get into graduate school. I was very much involved in activities and to some extent the social scene. I remember dancing to Count Basie live, in a huge ballroom, even though my lack of coordination was every bit as great in dancing as in athletics.

In my senior year I was asked to take charge of Religious Evaluation Week, which was rather a big deal on that Methodist campus. A close friend of mine and I came up with what we thought would be a blockbuster theme, "Let's Evaluate the Hell out of Religion." It would have been a bit controversial but might have drawn great crowds and quite possibly some spirited discussion.

Why this theme? My friend the philosophy major thought it would be fun. By this time, I had come to think of the hell-fire aspect of religion in about the same way I thought of the inherent discrimination in Greek fraternity life. And neither one of us were beyond provoking the leading administrators of our school.

As you can well imagine, we were ahead of our time. The administration took over the event and invited a Methodist minister from Ohio to be the keynote speaker. And then they changed the name of the event from Religious Evaluation Week to Religious Education Week. It was DePauw's loss, but my gain. I was ready to move on.

By the end of my junior year at DePauw I had begun to feel burned out from campus activities and was eager to take on some serious study. I started thinking about graduate school and had three things going for me. I had done well in my math courses, I tested well, and I was in a small cohort of students who would be applying. I was born in 1933, which year recorded the lowest number of U.S. births in a generation. An economist would characterize this as a cohort in short supply.

This was likely an aid in getting both the scholarship to DePauw and then financial aid for graduate school as well. I liked to think of it as my parents' reward for having the courage to have children during the depression, but then courage might have had nothing to do with it. Rather than courage, it may have been that my parents just failed to make the same rational decision that so many others did in the depths of the depression. I am grateful of course that for at least once reason lost out to passion.

I was ready for graduate school but needed financial aid. My record wasn't strong enough for the top tier but I did get some offers from good schools. The choice came down to Northwestern or Brown and I found the desire to go further east a powerful draw. I still wanted to explore new areas.

Now I Want to be an Academic

The years at Brown (1955-59) were good years. I took the work seriously and did well in my courses. I had no idea on entering Brown that I might want an academic career. All I knew was that I wanted some time for study prior to taking a real job. But then I liked the work as a graduate assistant in a statistics lab and I enjoyed teaching once I got my own class in the third year there. The idea of an academic life was growing on me.

I did have a bit of fun at Brown, most particularly in visiting the track at Lincoln Downs. I was going with a young woman whose uncle was president of the track so we were able to see the horses in the barns before placing our bets. We only bet a few dollars but once in a while won enough for dinner. The experience at the track did teach me that neither our observation of the ponies nor the recommendations found in the racing forms (the tout sheets) were of any value in predicting winners, and this led me to wonder whether the same might be said for picking winners in the stock market.

After a year at Brown I was given a summer fellowship to spend some time on Wall Street. I stayed in Greenwich Village and one night went to a theater called Circle in the Square, where I saw Jason Robards, Jr. in *The Iceman Cometh*. (This was while the theater was on Bleecker Street, prior to its moving to midtown Manhattan.) I was gaining a bit of culture. But I spent more evenings in lower Manhattan in a place called John Petersen's Fireside Inn, where with other guys in the Wall Street program[iv] we talked and drank Moscow mules. I did pick up enough from the Wall Street sessions to further my interest in financial markets, most particularly in how we deal with risk and uncertainty.

A course with Hyman Minsky further whetted my appetite for financial markets. Minsky assigned a paper on the question, "Does a Big Boom Mean a Big Bust?" He was just beginning to develop his financial instability hypothesis in which he asserted that stability breeds instability through leading us to underestimate risk and take on excessive debt. Minsky wrote extensively on this over the years until his death in 1996, but his work was largely ignored until the global financial crisis in 2008 made it all too relevant.

I was a skinny kid at Brown and Minsky was a big bear of a man who must have weighed about 250 pounds. He wore a brown sweater and looked exactly like the stuffed bear in a cage at Brown. He would take me out for ice cream, telling me he had to fatten me up. Thanks, Hy. I liked the company, and I liked the ice cream, but in retrospect I would have preferred to stay skinny for as long as I could.

In my fourth year at Brown I received a fellowship from the Ford Foundation, which gave me the time to work on a thesis with no grading or teaching responsibilities. Brown thought that should give me enough time to finish the thesis and my department made it clear that Brown would provide no financial aid after four years. I did have a thesis topic by my fourth year, on risk and the capital structure of the firm, but progress was slow. I wanted a teaching job but found myself interviewing without a convincing case that the thesis was nearly done.

By June I still did not have a job offer. But then I got a call from a small school in Ohio, went out for an interview, was offered a job, and jumped on it. The department was a small one, with five positions including two empty slots and one person on leave. They hired three of us in that fall of 1959, all of us on one-year contracts but anticipating that we would be asked to stay on. Just before Thanksgiving the three of us put our heads together and realized that only two of us would be asked to stay.

This was a bit unsettling. I told the chair that I needed to know my status and would have to plan to attend the meetings of the American Economic Association in Washington in late December (the job-market fair). After about three weeks I did get an offer to stay on but by that time had made arrangements to go to the meetings.

So it was a relaxed trip to the job market. I could stay where I was, with an offer in hand, but under the circumstances felt no obligation to do so. Unbeknownst to me, Boston College was in the market for economists.

Walsh, McEwen, and Bourneuf

In February 1958 Boston College embarked on a major change in direction with the naming of Michael P. Walsh, S.J., as its new president. B.C. at the time was largely a commuter school for first-generation college students from Irish and Italian families in the Boston area. It had a good faculty but nearly forty percent were Jesuit priests and many of the others had been Boston College undergraduates.

Walsh's goal was to transform Boston College into a major national university. This meant accelerating dormitory construction, which was already underway, so as to recruit students from throughout the country. It would mean a new approach to faculty hiring so as to make Boston College less insular. And Walsh's vision would mean building Ph.D. programs, so as to better attract leading scholars. The latter would have to be done selectively, since Ph.D. programs were expensive.

The Economics Department was chaired by a young Jesuit named Robert McEwen, in whom Walsh had great confidence. Walsh sounded out McEwen and in early 1959 told him to get going on a Ph.D. program—the resources would be there. The department did have a fledgling Ph.D. program, with three or four degrees granted to date, but the program was not a recognized one.

McEwen had the resources and he had the drive, but he knew he needed help. He called Paul Samuelson at M.I.T., told him his task, and asked if he could recommend someone to help. Samuelson was the leading economist of his time and was to become the first American to be awarded the Nobel Prize in Economics.

Samuelson told McEwen, "There is this woman named Alice Bourneuf. I know her from graduate school and from continued contact. She is at Berkeley, but she comes from a large Catholic family in Newton. She might be very interested in helping you build a Ph.D. program. She is a handful, but she is very good." McEwen sounded out others and got much the same response. He made Bourneuf an offer sight unseen, and she accepted.

Alice Bourneuf had been a graduate student at Harvard (or at Radcliffe, since Harvard did not admit women) with Samuelson and others who would become giants in the field. It was the late 1930s, with the world mired in depression and with Keynes having just published his masterwork.[v] Economics was exciting and challenging, and

18

econometrics that had become the heart of U.S. Ph.D. programs.

De Roover was a proud man and he sensed that he was being pushed aside by McEwen and Bourneuf as they took the program in a new direction. It was bad enough to become second fiddle, but to lose the limelight to a woman was particularly galling. To give a sense of what was happening, let me recount just two conversations with Raymond de Roover in my first year at Boston College.

We were talking at the circulation desk of the library, when he said, "Me, I'm an economist. That Bourneuf, she plays the numbers game." Change was coming, and it was hard for him. To de Roover, he himself was a natural fit for Boston College. He was integrating scholastic thought with classical economics, whereas Keynes was a sideline distraction, like a fly to be whisked away. The moderns, pursuing math-based theory and econometrics, had it all wrong.

On another occasion, as I was chatting with de Roover, he said, "They say I'm arrogant. Why, I'm not arrogant. I talk to you." Then he realized how that must have sounded, and he added, "Oh, but I'm a professor, and you're an instructor." And he meant it. He was friendly to me, but there was a matter of rank.

De Roover took his case to our president, Michael Walsh, and he threatened to take it to Rome on the grounds that this Jesuit, McEwen, and this woman, Bourneuf, were ruining an economics program that was rooted in Catholic tradition. He, de Roover, was the foremost scholar of economics in the Catholic tradition. The moderns, pursuing theory and econometrics, had it all wrong. He confronted Michael Walsh and gave him an ultimatum, "Either that woman goes or I go." Walsh said good-bye and wished him good luck.

It would have been great to keep de Roover, scholar that he was, but it could not be done if we were to build a Ph.D. program that would command respect throughout the profession. De Roover left for Brooklyn College in the summer of 1961 and when his book on the Medici was published in 1963 its preface made no mention of Boston College. It was said that a few years later, when Bourneuf took a leave to spend a semester at M.I.T., that de Roover exclaimed, "Ah I have been vindicated. The Vatican has removed her." Bourneuf of course returned to Boston College and the results of her research were published in our most prestigious journal, *The American Economic Review*.

I was told by a colleague some years later that at a conference de Roover had asked an M.I.T economist whether the people at M.I.T. read his work. When he got a less than encouraging response, he retorted, "They will be reading it fifty years from now." I am not sure that is the case at M.I.T., but at Boston College in 2013, fifty years following the comment, I was talking about De Roover's work in my course called "History of Financial Crises."

With de Roover's departure, it was clear sailing. McEwen and Bourneuf pursued the best people they could get, regardless of race or sex, at a time of rampant discrimination. By 1970 two out of seven of our full professors were women, and this was rare, since at that time women constituted only 5% of Ph.D.'s in economics. Our own graduate program had a larger share of women

Classroom Prayer

It was September 1960, just three months after I had arrived. I had prepared my syllabi and was ready for the semester. The Friday before classes were to begin we had a huge cocktail party in the auditorium of Campion Hall. The Jesuits really did know how to throw a party. There was shrimp on ice and every kind on booze one could imagine. I had consumed a few drinks and was standing talking with Bourneuf, McEwen, and a few others. Someone said to me, "Harold, I am not sure you knew this, but at Boston College it is customary to begin the classes with prayer. I blurted out, "Prayer? To Whom?"

Why such a response? Perhaps it was my Lutheran background telling me that these Catholics prayed to Mary and we Lutherans would never dream of doing that. Perhaps it was just the booze leading to an insensitive remark. McEwen patted me on the arm and said, "Harold, you don't have to do it."

I asked about the process and was told that at the beginning of class the bell would ring, the students would stand, and the instructor would lead them in prayer, with the students joining in. I thought about it over the weekend and decided what I would do.

On Monday, as I awaited my first class, the students were filing in and I was standing behind the desk, waiting for the bell. The bell rang and the students stood up, just as predicted. I told them my name, that I was new here and that I understood it was customary to begin the classes with prayer. I then told them that I was not going to lead them in prayer but that if they would like to have the prayer one of them should lead it and the others could join in as they choose. One of them did lead the prayer and it continued throughout the semester.

I had four classes and made the same announcement in each one. In two of them we had the prayer throughout the semester and in two we did not. I was okay with the idea of prayer but was not happy with the way it was done. The students would rattle off the "Our Father," or the "Hail Mary," without thinking about what they were saying, and late students would walk in while it was happening.

One day I said to the class after the prayer, "Now see here, I don't care whether you have the prayer or not, but if you do have it I want you to show some respect to those for whom it means something. Show a little reverence, and if you are late wait silently until it has concluded."

The prayer got better, at least for a few weeks, and I didn't think much more about it. Then about a year later I heard that one of the students had told a Jesuit that this young instructor had said something in class that had more impact than any sermon he had heard in a year. The story had gone through St. Mary's Hall (the Jesuit residence) and as it turned out stood me in good stead when a rather scandalous rumor began to circulate early in the spring semester.

I Meet my Bride

The first people I met at Boston College, in June 1960, were Bourneuf and McEwen. The next was a young woman behind the circulation desk of the library in Fulton Hall. Alice Bourneuf introduced her to me and told me how marvelous she was if I needed any help in finding materials. That young woman was Candy, and I was smitten from the very first day. The business library, which housed the books and periodicals for business and economics, was in Fulton Hall on the same floor as my office.

My office was in the west end of the building, the library was in the center and both the drinking fountain and the men's room were in the east end. I believed in drinking a good deal of water and so would walk by the library several times a day. Candy told me after we were married that she had wondered why I had to go to the men's room so often.

The library had exactly the materials I needed for my Ph.D. research—the thesis was not yet completed—so I did stop frequently at the desk. I was using the big red Moody's manuals, and they were reference works, so they could only stay out for three days. I didn't pay much attention to that, since I knew that no one else would want them over the summer. But then Candy began appearing at my door to remind me that they were reference works and they had to be back within three days.

One day at noon I ran into her outside of Fulton. We talked for an hour and then I asked her to lunch. She told me her lunch hour was up. I responded, "Well, how about dinner, tonight or perhaps tomorrow?" So the next night we went to dinner and then to summer theater on the Charles. We were engaged by November and married the following June.

I am going to share just a few lines from something I wrote for her on the occasion of our fiftieth wedding anniversary.

It seems like only yesterday
That I had come from far away
To find you there in Fulton Hall
A world so large and yet so small

I saw you there behind the desk
And I was really quite perplexed
I hadn't thought to find a bride
But all reserves were swept aside

It started with the reference works
You wouldn't give me special perks
They had to be back within three days
You told me I should mend my ways

And then one day out in the sun
We talked and talked just on and on
When I finally asked you out to lunch
Your hour was up so thanks a bunch

But then to dinner the very next night
And summer theater to set things right
We sat in a tent beside the Charles
For one of Shakespeare's lively brawls

It goes on from there but you get the gist of it. Candy and I were pretty much inseparable from that day onward and by November we were engaged. We set the wedding date for June, with plans to be married at All Saints

McEwen and Walsh knew that there would be a culture shock.

Another practice that I found objectionable was a proctoring assignment that came around at the end of both the first and second semesters. I was asked to proctor not only my own exams, of which I had four, but also to proctor for a large class in philosophy. I was a bit surprised by this but accepted it, at least in part because I had already done enough damage in that year.

But in my second year, when my colleague Mike Mann came on board, we talked together about how "unreasonable" this seemed to be. We had been brought on to build a graduate program in economics, and here we were, being asked to proctor exams in philosophy. We decided we would refuse the assignments and so notified the registrar, Eileen Tosney. (I have a copy of the letter I sent to her, in which I suggested that perhaps they might hire graduate students to proctor.)

Poor Eileen Tosney, not knowing what to do, talked to the dean of the college, John McCarthy, S.J. I was told later that Fr. McCarthy was apoplectic on hearing the news. Who did these young upstarts think they were? McCarthy of course called our chair, McEwen, and blasted him for having hired us in the first place. McEwen managed to calm him down a bit, with some comments on disruption as Boston College brought in more people from outside.

McEwen had Walsh's backing, and those of us in Economics were no longer asked to proctor outside the department. McEwen did suggest to Mike and me that it might have been better to tip him off on what we were about to do. As I reflect back on this, and some other bombs we threw in those first few years, it occurs to me that Michael Walsh wanted us to shake things up, that this was part of the plan, but perhaps not quite in that way.

The Bookstore Committee

As time went on I learned a bit about how to get things done without making people angry. Both Michael Walsh and Robert McEwen were Jesuits to the core but were also wily Boston politicians who knew how to pick your pocket and have you thank them for it. My first administrative assignment was as chair of the bookstore committee in early 1969. Seavey Joyce was president by this time and he needed someone to deal with recurrent complaints concerning the bookstore. Professors complained that the books they ordered weren't on the shelves in the number requested, and the bookstore director responded that professors weren't making the students buy books they had ordered, so he would make his own judgment on what would sell, thank you very much.

The students complained that the prices were too high, and the director responded that the theft rate was high, to which the students replied that the theft rate was high because the prices were outrageously high. I knew without Fr. Joyce's telling me that my job was to get the bookstore director replaced, and that I had to get this from a committee that included the director as a member of the committee.

The director was a long-time Jesuit of some standing, John E. Murphy, S.J., who was also Business Manager of the University and had a number of other roles. He was hard-working, energetic, and remarkably efficient, but he was perhaps not quite in tune with the faculty that had arrived in the past ten years.

Fr. Murphy could be abrupt and intimidating. He also ran the Campus Press, on which we depended to get multiple copies of things we might need to have reproduced. Faculty were unhappy but were reluctant to openly criticize him for fear of not getting what they needed in a timely fashion.

I sensed that the committee's task was to persuade Fr. Murphy that all of his duties were too much for one person, in a growing university, and that his other responsibilities were far more important. He did not give way easily. We on the committee were all on board with a number of recommendations, but we had one dissenter on the question of whether we needed a bookstore manager with that job as a sole responsibility. You can guess who that was.

Finally, I scheduled a meeting of the committee at my home and opened a bottle of wine, and then a second one. It was good wine. At the end of the meeting we had unanimous agreement on all issues, including the major one. I quickly finished the report, asked the members of the committee to give me comments if they had any reservations, and then sent it along to the president. (I wonder if it is too late to bill Boston College for the wine.)

Joyce was grateful—he in fact praised the report and urged it be sent to key administrators and the entire faculty--and that stood me in good stead when I became chair of economics two years later, in the midst of a financial crisis. I like to think I had learned a bit from the masters, Walsh and McEwen, and I discovered that it was more fun this way.

Ignatian Spirituality

As time went on, I adapted to the culture, or perhaps the culture adapted to me and the other young upstarts who were coming in. But one important aspect of Boston College that was always there became an important part of my life. That was a deep and growing respect both for the Ignatian tradition and Ignatian spirituality.

The Ignatian tradition of higher education takes second place to none. And Ignatian spirituality grounds one in the world with the loving presence of a higher power. I won't try to explain this in depth. Let me just give you a few principles from the *Pocket Guide to Jesuit Education*[viii] that had a profound impact on me. Be attentive. Pay attention to what is happening in your own life, that of those around you, and of the larger world. Be reflective. Look for patterns in what you observe, look for meaning, and look for cause and effect. And be loving. Do what you can to make the world a better place.

And finally, be involved. Don't just pray from the cloister; pray as did Dorothy Day by making the soup.

less rapidly than did the lay presence, and also less rapidly than the size of the student body. Total enrollment over the decade grew from 7410 to 9729, or by 31%.[x]

I don't have good numbers on how many of the new faculty had been Boston College undergraduates, but my impression is that there were not many over that period. Boston College had been turned down for Phi Beta Kappa in 1963 and one of the reasons given for the rejection was that "nearly one half of the faculty are Boston College alumni." In a response by Boston College it was pointed out that this number had declined from 58% in 1958 to 44% in 1963-64.[xi]

I recall a meeting of the local AAUP chapter in the mid-sixties in which a member of the faculty expressed concern over what he saw as discrimination against those who for so long had been the backbone of the school. He said, "If you are from Boston, are a BC graduate, and are Catholic, you have three strikes against you." It wasn't quite that extreme, but it might have seemed that way to some. In economics, Bourneuf and McEwen did hire one person who fit all three of the above categories in fall 1961, my esteemed and much-beloved colleague Frank McLaughlin, and he was brought in under Bourneuf and McEwen's determination to hire the best people they could. Frank was just too good to pass up.

I think it fair to say that there was a determined effort under Walsh to become less insular and that this did move us toward a much more diverse faculty. By the end of the Walsh decade, the theology department had moved from a faculty of 26, all of whom were Jesuits, to a faculty of 30, of whom 24 were Jesuits and 6 were not.

The social sciences showed particularly rapid growth over the ten-year period 1958 to 1968. The full-time faculty in Psychology rose from five (with two Jesuits) to fifteen (still with two Jesuits). Sociology grew from five (with one Jesuit) to nine (with no Jesuits). Political Science became a separate department (it had been a part of what in 1958 was called History and Government.) McGuinn Hall was completed in 1968 to house the School of Social Work and the above-named growing departments.

Economics moved from Fulton Hall to Carney Hall in 1963 and I recall how delighted I was to see how small the offices were. I would no longer have to share an office. Economics grew over the Walsh years from a faculty of nineteen (with five Jesuits) to a faculty of twenty-seven (with four Jesuits).

With a faculty growing much faster than the student body, and in particular with an increasing share of non-Jesuit faculty (whose salaries would not be turned back to the university), budget pressures began to develop by the end of the Walsh era, which pressures would explode in a financial crisis very early in the Joyce years.

New England Province of Jesuits did have a new provincial by this time and this may have made a difference in the ease of implementation.

This was a huge change for Boston College, but I don't recall thinking so at the time. Perhaps this was because all of my experience in education prior to Boston College had been coeducational and so I saw this as the norm. Perhaps it was because opposition to earlier efforts to admit women had cooled and by now we had near unanimity on the issue. Or perhaps my failure to note the import of the action was because in that spring I was deeply involved in other issues. The timing of the decision was fortuitous, since it gave Boston College an enlarged applicant pool as we weathered the financial crisis that was to come over the next four years.

The UAS and ROTC

The summer of 1969 was relatively calm. Joyce had put the Mary Daly case behind him, coeducation was on track, the bookstore had a new manager, and the tuition was set at a level that Joyce believed to be sufficient. The nation was relatively calm, at least in comparison with the prior summer, and so was Boston College.

I was focused on what I might do, individually or with others, in response to the tensions that were tearing our society apart. In the prior eighteen months we had been through the assassinations of Martin Luther King, Jr., and then of Bobby Kennedy. We had seen the riots that tore our cities apart and the disruption of the Democratic Convention in Chicago. We were faced with the realization that we had deep divisions along racial lines not just in the Southern United States but throughout the country.

I was active in my Church in forming what we called our "Urban Action Committee" and I had been involved in Fair Housing in my town of Brookline. As one thing I might do at Boston College, I had offered to teach a course in the Black Studies program if we had no one else in Economics to do so. The Vietnam War was continuing to accelerate and ROTC was an issue on the college campus.

Shortly before classes were about to resume, I received a phone call from Prof. Donald White, a senior colleague in Economics. Don was calling from Round Hill, that magnificent Jesuit retreat house in Dartmouth, Mass., looking out onto Buzzard's Bay. The University Academic Senate was there on a retreat to prepare for business of the coming year. There was an open seat on the Senate and Don wanted the group to appoint me. Moreover, he wanted me to co-chair with him the Committee on Curriculum. The group would be dealing with ROTC that coming fall and he wanted me there.

I was intrigued at the thought of being on the UAS--a policy-making group on which the faculty had some muscle, albeit with students and administrators, and I was flattered. I was a newly tenured associate professor, tenured by the skin of my teeth and with some heavy pushing by Don White. So I wasn't about to say no to Don. I jumped at the chance.

The Vietnam War had escalated throughout the decade, initially with widespread support but by now with growing concern. I had supported Presidents Kennedy and

Johnson, convinced by the domino theory (that if Vietnam fell to communism, then all of Southeast Asia would fall), but by now I too was opposed to the war.

On college campuses, ROTC was seen as a visible symbol of the war and it should be no surprise that anti-war sentiment coalesced around the presence of ROTC. Here I differed from my more strident anti-war friends, as did Don White. We took the position that our nation was going to continue to need our armed forces and if so we would be far better off with at least some of the officers trained at liberal arts schools rather than all at the military academies.

Boston College was a conservative campus, as schools go. Many of the students were first-generation college students, driven by a strong work ethic, patriotism, and a great desire to succeed. They had little use for the protestors they saw at Berkeley and Michigan. We did have radical students, of course, but they were far fewer in number at Boston College than at most of our universities. Thus we thought it possible to craft a compromise that would keep ROTC at Boston College.

Don and I worked for hours, with strong support from an outstanding student leader named Frank Dubreuil, and at a long night session in early December put the package together. It would retain ROTC on campus but would encourage it to use to the fullest extent possible courses approved for academic credit by departments outside of military science. Courses required for the program which failed to meet this condition would not be given academic credit. The proposal was brought to the UAS on December 14, 1969, and was approved by a vote of 44 to 2, with 4 abstentions. It was an overwhelming vote to retain ROTC at Boston College. We thought the issue was settled, but little did we know.

Financial Problems and the Tuition Strike

Tuition had been increased by $400, or 25%, as of September 1969 in the hope that this would bring in sufficient revenue to balance the budget for that year and the next. But then in December the President and the Trustees received the audited financial statements for Fiscal 1969 (the year just ended). The statements showed an operating deficit of $4.6 million, of which $1.6 million was made up by endowment income, annual giving, and contributed services of the Jesuit community. The remainder was covered by accumulated reserves, which by this time were almost depleted.

The president released the report to interested parties, including members of the U.A.S., and in an accompanying memorandum indicated that we could anticipate a similar operating deficit for the current year, fiscal 1970. Costs had risen as much as revenue and this time, 1969-70, there was precious little in reserves to make up the deficit.

To pay the bills we were borrowing from the Newton-Waltham Bank. The interest rate was the prime rate, which at that time was nearly 8%, and the notes were demand notes, which meant that repayment could be demanded at any time. Boston College was in a precarious financial position. The deficit would have to be cut. There was little that could be done in the current academic year, since faculty salaries were contractual for the year, and administrative salaries had in effect been promised for the rest of the year.

But for the following year the gap would have to be closed. There were just three choices--cut costs, increase revenue, or continue to borrow at a dangerous rate.

I don't know whether there was any serious consideration of cutting costs. I can report than in my department, Economics, we hired two people in the spring of 1970 to replace two who were leaving. Bear in mind that this was under F.X. Shea, Richard Hughes and Charles Donovan, when Economics had pretty much lost its clout with the administration. I can also report that in the spring of 1970 I personally received a salary increment for the following year of 14.6%, and I don't recall that I had any strong bargaining power. This is just anecdotal evidence, of course, but it suggests to me that neither the trustees nor the president saw cost cutting as the way out.

What the trustees did do was to authorize the president to increase tuition for the following year by an amount ranging from $200 to $500. Father Joyce opted for the full $500.

This meant that a junior who had elected to come to Boston College at $1600 per year with an expectation that it would move to $1800 for junior and senior years was already paying $2000 and would now be asked to pay $2500 for senior year. This was 56% more than the entering rate and was 39% more than the junior had expected to pay. A sophomore who had come in at $1600 and was now paying $2000 would be down for $2500 in junior year. Many of the students believed that in acceding to the large increase the prior year they had been promised there would not be another increase this year.

Seavey Joyce and his executive vice president Frank Shea met first with student leaders and then on April 8, 1970, Fr. Joyce held a large open forum to present the case for the tuition increase. The students objected--it appeared to them that they were being asked to simply pay the bill with no efforts having been made to cut costs, and in the course of the meeting they began to stamp their feet and call "Strike! Strike! Strike!"[xiv]

A strike committee was assembled by the undergraduate government and the strike began on Monday, April 13. Students manned the gates to the campus and stopped cars attempting to enter. Faculty were urged to turn around or if they did come on campus to support the strike. Occasionally cars were rocked a bit but none were overturned. Students were urged not to attend class and classes which were held were disrupted by blaring noise in the corridors. I recall trumpets and big bass drums in the halls of Carney. Within a few days virtually no undergraduate classes were being held in any meaningful way. Many of us continued to go to our classes but very few students came. There was little to do but to talk about the strike.

Negotiations continued but with little success. The President's office was occupied by students and undergraduate classes were at a standstill. (Graduate classes for the most part continued to meet.) At about the end of April a compromise was crafted under which tuition would rise by $240 and students would gain leverage in the decision-making process, particularly with representation on the budget committee. The leaders of undergraduate government endorsed the compromise, subject to a student referendum, and a vote was scheduled for the following Tuesday, May 5.

The Strike becomes a Strike Against the War

Then on Monday May 4, 1970, four students at Kent State in Ohio were killed by National Guard troops who had been called in to restore order. The students had been protesting against ROTC as a symbol of U.S. militarism run amok and had gone beyond the boundaries of what was seen as legitimate protest. They had set their ROTC building afire and had gone into the town on a rampage of vandalizing cars and smashing store windows.

The governor of Ohio had called out the National Guard and the troops were patrolling the campus. On that fateful Monday morning those nineteen-year old guardsmen were facing those nineteen-year old students. There were rumors (unfounded) of students having guns and of snipers on the roofs. Students were advancing with rocks. The kids with rifles were scared. Someone felt threatened and fired. More shots rang out and four students were killed.

A picture on the front page of the New York Times showed a young woman looking up in anguish as she knelt by the body of a fallen student. It was one of those pictures that had a profound impact on the entire nation. It seemed to symbolize what this war in Vietnam was doing to our country. We all thought at the time that the person pictured was a fellow student at Kent State. It turned out that she was a 14-year old runaway from Florida who had come to where the action was.

That Tuesday morning, May 5, we all knew what had happened and that picture in the New York Times made it all too real. Students at Boston College had been urged to be on campus for the referendum and many of them gathered in the dust bowl.[xv] Seavey Joyce released a letter in which he castigated President Nixon for expanding the Vietnam War into Cambodia (the Cambodian incursion). Students were determined to express their dissent and by now they appeared to have the blessing of President Joyce. ROTC was still the most visible target.

The chant began on the dust bowl, laced with profanity, in a very strong anti-war message. The leaders called for a march on Roberts Center, which housed the ROTC offices, and they set off down the hill. President Joyce, aware of what was happening and in fact quite likely to happen in light of his letter that same day, had asked the army officers to lock the doors and to leave the premises. He did not want a violent confrontation. The students smashed open the doors, overturned desks, and destroyed files. Having trashed the offices, they returned to cheering crowds.

Students voted in their referendum that same day to accept most of a 19-point agreement which had been worked out concerning the tuition strike and to join what had now become a nation-wide strike opposed to U.S. policy in Cambodia and Vietnam. The tuition strike was over but we were still not conducting classes. And ROTC was once more the hot-button issue in terms of how students were to express their opposition to the war.

The next morning the University Academic Senate met to consider how to deal with grades for the semester. President Joyce received a standing ovation. He was now a hero rather than a villain, having shown leadership in his opposition to the war. Students presented a petition asking for a special meeting of the UAS to reconsider ROTC. It was agreed that the UAS would adjourn until that evening, when questions both of academic credit for the semester and the future of ROTC could be considered. Meanwhile, the faculty would meet in the late afternoon.

The evening session began with another standing ovation for President Joyce. Agreement was reached on academic work which for most students meant being graded a pass with full academic credit provided they were passing at the time the strike began on April 13. For a letter grade in any class they could complete such work as agreed to with the instructor of the class.

Then a motion was introduced to sever all ties with ROTC at Boston College. After a brief but heated debate the motion passed. The faculty was split on the issue but both the student and the administrative members of the Senate voted overwhelmingly in favor. A number of us thought it unseemly to vote with student leaders who the day before had trashed the offices of the ROTC, but our calls for postponement of the vote went unheard. It was a tumultuous time.

The strike ended, we completed the semester in a manner of speaking, and we held commencement. President Joyce had turned the tuition strike into a strike against the war, which strike itself ended with our decision to banish ROTC, and we got through the semester with a minimum of property damage and no one being seriously injured. President Joyce had won the support of student leaders but had lost the support of much of the alumni and the faculty. His presidency was all but over.

The Housing Shortage and the Mods

The financial problems continued. Having failed to get the $500 tuition increase, settling for $240 instead, we faced a continuing revenue shortfall. An effort was now made to cut costs, in late spring 1970, including an instruction from the Dean of Arts and Sciences to send notice of non-renewal to first-year instructors. The Arts and Sciences chairs rebelled on the grounds that this would be highly improper if not illegal and would severely damage faculty morale.

Throughout the spring, as it became increasingly clear that the tuition increase of $500 would not hold, we had focused on increasing enrollment. We were already admitting virtually all who applied as commuters, but we did have the possibility of taking additional resident students if only we could provide housing for them.

So we accepted additional students and promised them housing. Then we set out to find the housing, with executive vice president F.X. Shea in charge. Shea had honed his negotiating skills in dealing with the student strike and now he took on the city of Boston. He first reached an agreement to buy the Somerset Hotel in Kenmore Square, but the mayor vetoed it. So he turned to an apartment complex in Brighton called Towne Estates and made a substantial deposit. Residents objected and the mayor vetoed that one too.

It was now July and the students were coming in September with a promise of housing. So we turned to a firm in Connecticut that told us they could put modular housing in place by fall. We had checked with them as early as March but rejected the notion out of the belief that our students would not tolerate being asked to live in modular housing. How little did we know the tastes of our students.

I recall a meeting in McElroy in which Father Donovan (academic vice president) shared with faculty the news that we had found a solution to the housing problem. We were all a bit skeptical but saw it as acceptable given that we had no good alternatives. We would temporarily place students in hotels until the units were put in place in the course of the fall term. So we poured the foundations and awaited the trucks. The first one arrived in early October. A crane lifted it and was about to put it into place when it came crashing down. It was a time when things just did not seem to be going well. But it was replaced and more were installed over the next few months.

They leaked terribly in that first year and they were alternately too hot or too cold--they were poorly insulated. We replaced the roofs and put on new siding. None of us expected them to be there for more than five to ten years, but the students loved them and opted for them from the very beginning. What we saw as a trailer camp the students saw as on-campus apartments complete with a yard and a grill. We had begun the era of the mods.

The Black Talent Program

The fall semester of 1970 began with the mods under construction and students in hotels while they waited. We were all eager for a return to normal classroom work. One striking innovation of that fall was an all-Black dorm on upper campus, Fenwick Hall. Boston College had intensified its efforts to attract Black students, as had most schools in light of the Kerner report[xvi] following massive urban unrest. We had funded a Black Talent program, had added courses in Black Studies, and had brought on a director named A. Robert Phillips. Phillips saw his role as that of urging the Black students to take charge of their own lives at Boston College.

Many of the Black students had expressed a desire to share an all-Black dorm, coed but with women and men separated by floor. We were a bit chagrined, since our ideal was one of integration, but at the same time we sympathized with the view that being together in the living unit could offset some of the pressure that minority students experienced in the classroom and the dining hall. Fr. Joyce approved the dorm when it appeared the students might take it anyway after months of bickering within the administration as to whether we could approve an all-Black coed dorm. It was our first coed dorm and thus another forerunner of what was to come.

I had volunteered to teach a course called Black Economic Development in the U.S. and had done this for the first time in the prior spring--in the strike semester. I had thirteen students in the class, all Black and to the best of my recollection all freshmen. We struggled to make sense of a topic which would have been difficult even with prior background in economics.

One of my students was David Silvia, a young man of enormous leadership potential but who was struggling with some inner demons. He shot himself later that year and at his funeral I believe I got some sense of what had been going through his mind. He was caught up in the Black power movement but his parents, from the Cape Verde Islands, saw themselves as Portuguese. The people at the funeral were virtually all White. Something in the transition from that community to his world at Boston College was too much for David and a great leader was lost. For some years following we had the David Silvia award at Boston College, which was given each year to the "AHANA student[xvii] who has done the most to improve the quality of life for AHANA students."

I had talked to A. Robert Phillips a number of times in the fall of 1970 and had some sense of what he was trying to achieve with the Black Talent Program. What I didn't know was its financial condition until I got a call to come to Frank Shea's office at the end of November. Frank asked me and Al Folkard to come to his office to help him deal with an important issue. Al was the director of the A&S Honors program and was both a huge supporter and a confidante of many of the Black students. I had taught a course in the Black Studies program and was seen as having credibility throughout the university.

When we came to his office on Nov. 30, 1970, Shea told us that the Black Talent Program was in trouble. Its budget was a generous one, most particularly given the financial difficulties of Boston College, but Phillips had committed more than 2/3 of it to the first semester. It faced a substantial deficit for the spring. Shea told us a bit about his vision for the program.

Boston College's Black Talent program was to be different. All of the other schools were creaming the perceived best of the Black students. We were going to take the ones who if they were not here would be in jail or on the streets, and we would provide them with a first-rate college education. My immediate thought was "Thank God Phillips isn't listening to him. Phillips is getting the best students he can and a number of them are very, very good."

In retrospect, I think what Shea was trying to tell us was that Phillips would go beyond the usual routes to talent, such as guidance counselors, in an effort to find prospects that the Ivy schools had missed, and that he would waive the usual admissions standards to get someone good. A prime example of those he found was Julianne Malveaux, who was admitted to Boston College without a high school degree and then proceeded to compile an excellent record. I will have a bit more to say about Julianne later.

Fr. Shea told us that he was off the next day for a month's leave and would be out of touch. He wanted Al and me to look into the problem and recommend a solution to the president, Fr. Joyce.

Our first question of course was how Phillips could have spent so much of the money in the first semester. We found out. He wanted all of the students to see themselves as independent of their parents and to be all on the same footing. So they were all given full tuition, board and room, book money, and spending money. This included a few whose parents were quite wealthy and could easily have paid tuition. But Phillips saw these students as all in one boat together, as a group who were going to separate themselves from their parents and become new models of Black leadership. They were going to work hard both at academics and at leading the Black Talent program, and they were going to have the funds the do so.

When we asked Phillips how he expected to provide the students with the funds promised for spring term--the same as in the fall--he did not give us a direct answer. After a number of conversations I asked him to come to my house for dinner one night so we could talk some more. He accepted and then at the last minute called to tell me he couldn't come. His house had been broken into and he couldn't leave until the lock was repaired.

He asked me if I could come to his place in Roxbury that evening. He was testing me of course. He wanted to see if I would come. So I drove into Roxbury that evening and parked on a quiet street near his home. We talked at length and shared a bottle of wine, but we didn't get very far. He wanted more money for the program and he wanted the students to take over the program. He believed in their potential as leaders and saw this as a way for them to develop that potential. He believed the program needed the money he had committed and that the university would come up with it.

Al had been talking to Phillips as well--we had thought it might be productive for both of us to seek him out--and we had both been talking to the student leaders of the program. And we had talked to our new financial vice president and treasurer (John Smith) and to Boston College personnel in charge of admissions and financial aid.

It was now early January and it was time to report to Joyce. I took the position that the money had been promised the students for spring term and we would have to come up with it. Father Joyce said that if he went to the Board to ask for more money for the Black Talent Program they would cancel the program. He was probably right--the program was facing a huge cost overrun in the midst of a financial crisis at Boston College. Joyce made it clear that more money was not an option. Al Folkard said he thought he could work something out--he was very good at that--and he did.

The students took huge cuts for the spring term--they took out loans to meet expenses--and in return they were given control of the program. A. Robert Phillips resigned, having achieved what he wanted most of all, a Black Talent Program wholly under student control--admissions, financial aid, and budget. The B.C. directors of admissions and financial aid were extremely upset, as were a large majority of the faculty. I thought the resolution was a mistake--I did not think it wise to put students in charge of admissions for any program and I saw an obvious conflict of interest in their determining their own financial aid.

I still think it was a mistake but in retrospect I have to concede that the students did an excellent job in running the program. They went after the best students they could get and to the best of my knowledge their administration of the finances was scrupulously above board.

I mentioned that we had talked to John Smith. This was on December 28, 1970, John's first day on the job. We met him in his office--a cubicle in the back of Gasson 100, which was then the treasurer's office. He had an old desk and a broken chair. We gave him the news of the deficit in the Black Talent Program. John even then had a spirit of optimism, but it can't have been a very good first day. John went on of course to be a major factor in the recovery and resurgence of Boston College.

John Smith had been found at Raytheon Corporation and been named by Seavey Joyce to be Financial Vice President and Treasurer. This was one of three important appointments made by Seavey Joyce--the other two being Don White and Jack Maguire--all three of whom continued for years after Joyce had gone and made outstanding contributions. In looking back at the Joyce years we often forget that he did choose some superlative leaders. The appointments of Don White and Jack Maguire will be described in the coming pages.

The Search for a Graduate Dean

Samuel Aronoff had been named Dean of the Graduate School in 1969 but he only lasted two years in the job. Sam had come here from Iowa State as a Director of Research but he didn't understand either our culture or even what a Ph.D. really meant. I remember serving on the graduate educational policy committee with him and his asking one day, "What does it mean to be a Ph.D. in Economics? We are talking here about a doctor of philosophy. That must mean something. It must mean something that cuts across disciplinary lines."

I took the position that it meant the same thing it meant at Harvard or M.I.T. or Wisconsin--that it meant serious research with the standards and requirements as set in the discipline. With respect to requirements for a Ph.D., it would be far better to emulate the best programs than to cast about for something completely different. I had differences with Sam but still have a soft spot in my heart for him. On leaving he gave me for my office his Wang Computer, which at the time was a pretty sophisticated machine.

Sam resigned in spring 1971 and we had a search committee for a new Dean of the Graduate School. Seavey Joyce had learned a bit in terms of faculty reaction when he had named a new dean of Arts and Sciences two years earlier with no faculty consultation. This time a search committee of three faculty was named and I was a member of the committee. I have no idea why I was involved in so many of these committees. Perhaps it was simply because I continued to say yes when asked and possibly for some reason it was thought I had credibility with the faculty. Perhaps in this case it was primarily because I had complained about the selection process the last time around.

I remember that Gerry Bilodeau from the Math department was with me on the committee and another whose name I cannot recall. We had decided to limit the search to internal candidates and were to give three names to Dean of Faculties Fr. Donovan, who would then pass them along to Seavey Joyce. To Gerry and me, Don White was the obvious choice. He had the credentials both as a scholar and an administrator, he was a great negotiator, he cared about Boston College, and under certain conditions he was willing to take the job. We recommended Don White and in late July of 1971 we gave Fr. Donovan his name along with two others about whom at best we felt lukewarm. We crossed our fingers and hoped that Seavey would see that he really had only one viable candidate.

Seavey was not all that enchanted with the idea of Don White as graduate dean--the differences over ROTC and some other issues were still smoldering--but he did recognize Don's ability and his integrity. So he offered him the job. It was now that Don's negotiating skills came into full play. Don told Seavey he would accept if he might also be named Associate Dean of Faculties and effectively co-dean of Arts and Sciences.

Don prevailed and the appointment was made. He recognized that with no hiring or budget authority a graduate dean would have no influence. We were in a period of financial stress and Don rightly recognized that with the proper tools to work with he could be helpful. Don White was a key figure in maintaining programs in those difficult years and then in building them as momentum returned over the next twenty years.

A Search for Director of Admissions

It was a busy year. That same spring, 1971, I was also on a screening committee to choose a new Director of Admissions. Arthur Doyle, who had been appointed to the post just two years earlier, announced his resignation in May to be effective on July 1. I knew Arthur well and respected him as a highly competent professional who cared very much about Boston College. Al Folkard and I had talked to him at length the prior December and January concerning the Black Talent program and I know that even then he was upset at having admissions for the program removed completely from his jurisdiction. This was something Frank Shea had simply decided to do. Then when the program was turned completely over to student leadership, Arthur was even more concerned. Arthur had nothing but good things to say about Boston College on announcing his resignation, but I took his resignation as a statement that he could not in conscience continue without substantial changes in policy.

So we had a committee, chaired by Academic Vice President Charles Donovan,[xviii] and including John Mahoney from our English Department and me, along with a number of others. We came up with three candidates, all of them outsiders but all with experience in admissions. The job was offered to each in turn, but each one, on taking a closer look at Boston College at the time, decided to say no.

By now it was late July and we had no director of admissions. Fr. Donovan called in John Mahoney and me to ask for our help. He (Fr. Donovan) was about to leave for a month abroad and this couldn't wait until his return. Did we have any ideas as to who might be an interim director of admissions while we continued the search? We quickly suggested a colleague who was widely respected and whom we considered to be a good soldier who would likely take the job.

Fr. Donovan asked us to talk to him and if for some reason he were to say no then to do our best to find someone else and present our recommendation to Fr. Joyce. Our candidate said no--he no doubt had good reasons that I didn't quite understand, but he did go on in a few years to become a college president elsewhere. John and I quickly explored other possibilities. We talked to a number of people, looking for leads, including Bob Carovillano, chair of the Physics Department. Bob suggested Jack Maguire, an assistant professor of Physics who had broad university interests and was extraordinarily able.

John Mahoney and I then arranged to meet for lunch the next Tuesday at the Harvard Faculty Club and we talked about Jack. He had no experience in admissions but was intrigued at the possibility. (We had discussed it with him by now.) John knew him from Lexington, where Jack Maguire was chair of the school committee, and he could attest to Jack's administrative ability.

I knew Jack from a long ride together to the funeral of David Silvia a few months before, among other encounters, and I had great respect for him. Jack was bursting with energy and was eager to take on the challenge. We talked again at a meeting on John's front porch in Lexington, and we settled on Jack Maguire as our candidate. The next job was to present our recommendation to Fr. Joyce.

We met with Seavey Joyce on August 13. When he finally understood our recommendation, he nearly exploded. "What? You want me to take an assistant professor of physics and put him in charge of admissions? Are you crazy? Do you realize how important this job is?" My response was, "Who have you got?" We all settled down a bit and John and I told Fr. Joyce everything we knew about Jack. Fr. Joyce agreed to talk to him. They talked and Jack agreed to take it as an interim appointment on the condition he could at least be a candidate for the ongoing position.

Jack Maguire was an instant hit in admissions and he went on to become the guru of the college admissions process throughout the United States. He was the first to apply regression analysis to the question of college choice and to use quantitative methods in a sophisticated manner. He recruited excellent people who in turn went on to be directors of admissions at leading schools. John and I had no idea of course that Jack would be as successful as he was, but we did see some things in him that gave us confidence. Sometimes you need to go with your instincts and sometimes you get lucky.

The summer ended and by this time I was chair of the Department of Economics. John Smith and Jack Maguire were offering $500 off the tuition bill to any new commuting student who would come and we did get a few more. We increased tuition by $260 for 1971-72 and at the same time instituted a salary freeze. We thereby managed to balance the budget. But the short-term debt remained on the books, rolled over to the next year, and by June 1972 it was slightly in excess of the total value of our endowment.[xix]

Seavey Joyce's days as president were numbered and he resigned in January 1972. After a two-year leave he came back to teach in the Economics Department, where I was chair. He did a fine job in the classroom but was obviously uncomfortable as a former president still at Boston College. He left to become a parish priest in northern Michigan, where by all accounts he was a beloved priest. Frank Shea had resigned earlier to become president of St. Scholastica's in Duluth, Minnesota. Then he left the Jesuit order, got married, and left St. Scholastica's to go on to Antioch College.

My Take on the Joyce Years

The years 1968-1972 were difficult ones for any college president. They were years of tumult, with the escalation of the Vietnam War, riots in our inner cities, tensions following the assassinations of Martin Luther King, Jr. and Bobby Kennedy, and a growing awareness of the impacts of both racism and sexism in the United States. We also had a rapid rise in inflationary pressures for which our colleges were not well prepared.

Boston College had embarked on a Negro Talent Search in 1968, which within a year became the Black Talent Program. We had continued with graduate program expansion as begun under Michael Walsh. Both were expensive. In fall 1970 we became fully coed with the admission of women to the two schools which had theretofore been all male, Arts and Sciences and the College of Business Administration.

Financial controls at Boston College were at best very weak. President Joyce was told by his Financial Vice President in fall 1968 that he would need a tuition increase of $400 for 1969-70 but that should be sufficient to provide a balanced budget for both 1969-70 and 1970-71. By December 1969 he was given financial reports showing a large deficit for the year just ended, 1968-69, and projected as well for the current year.

It would not have been too late at that point to institute a hiring freeze for the following year or even a freeze on faculty salaries. Joyce elected instead to proceed with plans underway and to ask for an increase in tuition of another 25%, which would mean an increase of 56% over a two-year period. That proved to be his undoing.

There were some notable accomplishments under Seavey Joyce, including the aforementioned Black Talent Program and admission of women, reform of the core curriculum in a way that cut requirements and yet maintained a respectable core (even as a number of schools were dismantling their core programs), and appointment of such outstanding leaders as Financial Vice President John Smith, Director of Admissions Jack Maguire, and Graduate Dean Donald White. All three would survive the Joyce administration and prove to be immensely valuable over the next twenty years.

But Joyce had also appointed Frank Shea as his executive vice president. Shea had been a popular teacher but he had no administrative experience and as it turned out had limited skills in negotiation. His style was confrontational and he managed to alienate far too many people. Shea persuaded Joyce to appoint Richard Hughes as Dean of Arts and Sciences with no real consultation of the faculty and without employing a search committee of any kind.

And Joyce failed to immediately rein in costs when he was given the news in December 1969 of continued deficits. Had he instituted an immediate hiring freeze with a modest increase in tuition for the following year, rather than asking for a 25% jump in tuition for the second year in a row, his tenure might have been much different.

Joyce left office with reserves depleted and short-term debt in excess of the endowment. A large number of faculty were upset over perceived capitulation of the president to radical students, and many in Arts and Sciences were continuing to smolder over having been given a dean as an administrative appointment rather than through a search committee.

When Frank Shea resigned the general attitude was one of relief. When Joyce resigned the attitude was more one of sorrow that things had not gone better for him. We did know it was time for him to leave, and we looked forward with a mix of trepidation and hope.

My Own Story over Years 1960 to 1972

I came to Boston College with major interests in capital markets and in statistics, but I had not had graduate courses in either field. The program at Brown in 1955-59 was very small and did not offer those courses. I was learning capital markets on the fly but was not prepared to teach graduate-level statistics.

I suspect that Bourneuf and McEwen sensed this and wanted to help prepare me. They brought in a visiting professor from M.I.T. who gave a small number of us a wonderful tutorial in statistics in my first year, 1960-61. This gave me both the ability and the confidence to teach graduate statistics in my second year and for some years following. My most notable memory of teaching that course in my second year was that the Jesuit provincial showed up one evening to sit in on a class. He didn't say anything, either during or after the class, but I suspect he was pretty bored.

I was brought to Boston College to help build a Ph.D. program and one of the expectations was a high level of research and publication. It took me a long time to admit that in this I was less than successful. Okay, I was a failure. It took me four years following Brown to finish my Ph.D. thesis. I had worked with it off and on for five years, including a year at Brown, but was not happy with what I had. Then early in 1963 my thesis advisor called me and said, "Harold, I want you to finish by this spring. Bring me a completed draft within six weeks." I did so, got comments, made revisions, and then spent the spring break typing the final copy.

The thesis was completed, and an abstract of it was published both in the *Journal of Finance* and in a book of readings. I wrote a paper based on the thesis and submitted it to our top journal, the *American Economic Review*. The paper was rejected, with comments that could have made it better. But I thought it was pretty good as it was and threw it in a drawer. In retrospect, I should have taken the comments seriously and I should have reached out to colleagues for help.

I wrote other papers but they were not accepted as submitted, and I never quite got around to revising them. Or perhaps I was unwilling to do so. Or I was too involved in other things. Or I just wasn't very good at tailoring papers for publication. At any rate my research career was far from stellar and the tenure decision was approaching.

In 1964 I was asked to participate in a study of the role of the futures market in determining the price of sugar. I did a chapter investigating whether movements in the price of sugar were evidence of a speculative bubble, which might have been furthered by the futures market, or might be due to a series of random events that just happened to be reducing the outlook for future supply and thus kept pushing up the price. The chapter was really quite good, if I do say so, and the study of the market was published in book form.

I gather this book, written jointly with others, was sufficient to meet the research requirement for tenure, but the case was clearly less than overwhelming. I had prepared myself for being turned down and was looking at other options when I learned that tenure had been granted. I know Don White pushed the case for me very hard, as did Bourneuf and McEwen, but I couldn't imagine why any reasonable person would have done so in light of my record in research. Had I been a member of the promotions committee looking at a similar dossier, I am sure I would have voted no.

The signal I was given on being tenured was that there was some hope my research career would still take off, but that even if it did not I would have value in other areas. I wasn't too sure what those might be, and I was embarrassed when people asked me about my research. It took me a long time to realize that failure to deliver in one aspect of expectations is not failure as a person, and it took me some time to deposit my paycheck without a sense of guilt. I stayed on because I had a family to feed, I really did like the academic life, and I continued to believe that at some point I would have work that would be published.

I did have positive affirmation outside of Boston College, both through my church and in the larger community. Most of this was through involvement in the burgeoning civil-rights movement of the sixties and seventies, and this involvement was a natural lead-in to my participation in the Black Studies Program at Boston College.

In 1965, when Martin Luther King, Jr. led the march from Selma to Montgomery, most of us thought that the racial divide in the U.S. was largely in the South. Then later that year we had a major civil disturbance in Watts, followed in 1966 by one in Chicago and in 1967 in Newark. Then in July 1967, just two weeks following the riot in Newark, we had a particularly violent eruption in Detroit which left 43 dead and hundreds injured. This one required intervention by the National Guard and by both the 82nd and 101st Airborne Divisions. It was now apparent that we had serious issues concerning race throughout the U.S. and not just in the South.

President Johnson appointed a group which came to be known as the Kerner Commission to determine what had happened, and why, and what might be done to keep it from happening again. The Kerner report, released in February 1968, concluded that "Our nation is moving toward two societies, one black, one white—separate and unequal."[xx] It said that a major cause of the urban riots was White racism, which led to discrimination in employment, education, and housing. The Commission recommended that both the private sector and the federal government take strong action to examine racism in America and then to end racial disparities.

The Kerner report was an immediate best seller, and it amplified efforts that were already under way in a number of our institutions. In February 1968 Boston College had launched what became its the Black Talent Program.

Also in February of 1968 I was involved in forming an "Urban Action Committee" in my church in Brookline. With the help of our Bishop, we received permission to install posters on racism on the MBTA trolley cars. The MBTA would let us do this with only a labor charge for installation, provided we delivered posters of the right size and shape. We came up with ideas, enlisted the help of a design firm in Cambridge, and found a printer. We had asked the MBTA to put them solely on the Green Line, because we wanted our focus to be on our neighbors in Brookline, Brighton and Newton, but they in fact appeared throughout the city and suburbs.

The first one to appear, in resplendent red, white and blue, read "a racist is someone who believes that America is already the land of equal opportunity." And then in smaller print, "concerned? contact The Urban Action Committee/All Saints Church Brookline." A second one, this one primarily green, read, "a racist is someone who believes in Civil Rights but knows you have to watch out for property values." The plan was to install two new ones every month, so that riders of the T might begin to wonder what was to come next. Bear in mind that this was well before smart phones, when riders of the T had little to do but read the paper or look at the advertising posters.

Three of us were actively involved in the project at first, but one of us moved away that summer and another became very busy. So I became the point person, delivering copy to the printer, picking up the posters and bringing them to the MBTA. And then I spent hours riding the T back and forth, both to see if indeed the posters did appear on the cars (they did) and to watch peoples' reaction to them. People often looked a bit puzzled, and I suppose some were angry, but I did not see any efforts to deface the posters or to tear them down. It had become fashionable to at least talk about racism in America if not to do anything about it. The posters continued to appear on the cars from November of 1968 through July 1969.

I had been a bit involved in Fair Housing in Brookline by the mid-sixties and had come to realize how nearly impossible it was to find a realtor who would show properties to Blacks. The realtors were of course reacting to pressures from owners and neighbors. I had moved from Brighton in the Cleveland Circle area to Brookline in 1967, in order to take advantage of the Brookline Schools. Then a former neighbor in Brighton, a Black professor at Boston College, tried to make a similar move in 1968. He wished to rent, as had I, and he had no success in even being shown apartments for rent.

A friend of mine who was active in Fair Housing became so concerned that he bought a two-family house with a vacant unit and took in the professor as a tenant. He then proceeded to establish a non-profit foundation called The Foundation for Brookline Housing, raised some money and had the foundation take over the two-family house. The goal of the foundation was to make housing more accessible to Blacks in Brookline, by buying two and three-family homes and renting the units to Blacks. The rents would be modest—just enough to cover costs, including mortgage costs, but without an equity return.

I persuaded my church to make a sizeable grant to the foundation and then was made a member of the Board and the treasurer of the group. Our purpose was clear—we wanted to see more Black children in our parks and playgrounds and to see their parents in our stores, churches, and restaurants. METCO had been busing children into the Brookline schools by this time but the kids went back home at the end of the school day. That wasn't the same as our goal of living together in community.

Initially we had hoped to have integrated housing units. But with our first one, the White upstairs neighbor was so angry, and so disagreeable, that we had to evict him. He was a bit of a town activist and began to spread stories about this group that was going to bring in an influx of Blacks and destabilize neighborhoods. In response we held open meetings in which we assured people we didn't have the resources to buy many properties and that those we did buy would be scattered throughout the town rather than grouped in any one neighborhood.

We replaced the upstairs neighbor with a second Black family and in other units purchased we rented only to Blacks. This was both to minimize confrontations between close neighbors and to use our resources to maximize the number of Black families brought into Brookline. Yes, we did practice discrimination, and the experience even then left me with mixed feelings, just as did my de facto discrimination at Boston College by teaching a class in our Black Studies program in which White students were not given a chance to enroll. It was not easy to reconcile the desire to get something done with a deep-seated abhorrence to making any selections on the basis of race.

So I came to involvement at Boston College in the years 1969-71, in the events described earlier, with a bit of perspective from my experience in Brookline, and I like to think this might have been helpful as we wrestled with the issues. My experience with the Foundation for Brookline Housing almost certainly made me a bit more receptive to the notion that incoming Black freshmen might be permitted to opt for an all-Black dorm and possibly to take one or two classes in which all of their fellow students would be Black.

I also had developed some experience in budgeting and finance, as treasurer of my church from 1966-1971 and also treasurer of the Foundation for Brookline Housing. This perspective may have been helpful as I became a member of the Boston College budget committee a bit later in 1978-82.

Part 3 - Resurgence and New Challenges

Monan to the Rescue

When J. Donald Monan became the 24th president of Boston College in August 1972, morale was low and the debt was staggering. But John Smith was on board, and John was not only a brilliant financial administrator but also an eternal optimist. Don White was the Associate Dean of Faculties and was a person who could mediate disputes and do more with a tight budget than anyone else. Jack Maguire was beginning to work his magic with applications and enrollment. Within a year Monan appointed Frank Campanella to be his executive vice-president. Frank was not only extraordinarily capable but was also stable and reasonable as opposed to the mercurial Frank Shea.

In 1973 Monan appointed Thomas P. O'Malley, S.J., as Dean of Arts and Sciences but only after two search committees had failed to yield acceptable candidates. Given that there had been two search committees, the faculty could hardly say that it had not been consulted.

I had been interviewed for the position of dean but had told the committee that there was no way I could be effective, given my record of research and publication. We needed someone with greater stature. Nonetheless, I was told that my name was one of those put forward by one of those committees. I was flattered but certainly understood Monan's judgment that search committees do not always produce acceptable results.

In December 1972, just months after taking office, Fr. Monan announced that the tuition increase for the following year would be just $50, and with this came a message that financial management would involve cost controls as well as tuition increases. Costs were controlled and we had a surplus for 1972-73.

Monan also encouraged the development of a faculty compensation committee which would write an annual report and then meet with university officials concerning salaries and benefits. We had begun something like that under Walsh, with an elected faculty committee that met with the president, but under Joyce this committee was replaced by the University Academic Senate. The UAS, comprised as it was of faculty, administrators, and students, did not provide a voice for the faculty as such.

Faculty were increasingly frustrated at the need for a voice. They began to gather as a caucus within the UAS in an effort to exercise some muscle. Members met with a committee of the Board of Trustees in February 1973 to discuss, among other issues, the determination of faculty compensation. Out of that meeting came a suggestion that there be a meeting each fall of faculty representatives with the president and other administrators to discuss faculty salaries and benefits.

Monan was receptive and the Caucus asked me to draft a report on compensation to be used as a basis for the fall discussion. The report was submitted in June 1973 by the Faculty Caucus, and that caucus itself morphed over time into the Faculty Compensation Committee, which continued to write reports and meet with administrators over the succeeding years.

Boston College had been reporting by fall 1971 that efforts by both Michael Walsh and Seavey Joyce to increase faculty salaries had been paying off. Faculty compensation at Boston College now compared quite favorably with the national average as revealed in numbers reported by A.A.U.P. (The American Association of University Professors had for some years been collecting and publishing data on faculty salaries and benefits throughout the nation.) We slipped a bit relative to others during the salary freeze year 1971-72, but the data still showed our compensation to be a bit above the average.

I pointed out in my report that when adjusted either for the high cost of living in the Boston area or for the higher average salaries across all professions in the Boston area, that salaries at Boston College were still very low and were not high enough to attract and retain the people we wanted. The report was well received, and I became the go-to person for data on faculty compensation over the next ten years.

Being a Chair under Joyce and under Monan

I became acting chair of economics in spring 1971 and then chair from 1971-78. In spring '71 the department was given permission to replace two out of four people who would be leaving at the end of the year. Salaries had been frozen for the coming year and we had been cut by two slots. My colleagues in the department told me we could not take the cuts and that I must stand up to the administration. Given the financial crisis, I thought it fortunate that we could hire at all. I told them I had pushed as hard as I could and in my judgment any more would be counterproductive.

A student contingent in economics had been urging me to hire a Marxist. I met with them and told them that we didn't even speak the same language as Marxists and would not be able to communicate. I asked them if they really wanted a Marxist, or if we might not approach someone who was interested in political economics and would take a highly critical approach to how the U.S. economic system functioned. They conceded as much, and we brought in Barry Bluestone, who as a graduate student at Michigan had been a member of URPE (the Union of Radical Political Economists).

The students loved Barry, as did we, and Barry continues to have a special place in my heart as my first hire. Barry's courses in Political Economy were a huge success and he gave us an added bonus in that he was willing to take on a large teaching load as we struggled to deal with the cuts in our faculty. Barry was a staunch liberal and by 1972 I had become a conservative. From 1972 through 1982 we had spirited debates preceding the presidential elections. Barry left in 1986 for an offer that was just too good to refuse, but he has stayed in touch and we have a continued warm relationship.

In the next year we hired Marvin Kraus and in succeeding years Joe Quinn and Kit Baum, all of whom have made major contributions to Boston College. We hired others as well who either left after a year or two or did not get tenure. We managed to retain Jim Anderson and Dick Tresch, who had been hired just before I became chair, and who were essential to the program. By the end my term as chair our number of faculty slots had fallen from 27 to 23. I was balancing demands from my colleagues to resist further cuts against the pressures throughout Boston College to constrain costs. I take some pride in that we were able to keep the ship afloat as we awaited better times.

The financial pressure continued for a number of years, but the job became more pleasant as the years went on. In my first year or two as chair, in the latter part of Joyce's presidency, I was met with frustration whenever I had to reach out to someone else, whether it be a matter of purchasing or personnel. The reaction I got was pretty much "What are you bothering me for? I have enough problems." Within a few years of Monan's arrival, the attitude throughout the university was completely different. The response had become "Let's see what we can do." I didn't always get what I wanted, but the entire interaction had become much more positive. There was a growing sense under Monan that we were working together to get back on track.

Bill Neenan Comes to Boston College

In early 1978, as I was about to finish my first term as chair, I received a letter from our academic vice president, as did all the chairs. Fr. Donovan told us that the Jesuit community had established an endowed chair to be known as The Gasson Chair. The purpose was to bring distinguished Jesuit scholars and teachers here for a year or two on visiting appointments. The chairs were invited to submit names. I paid no attention, being convinced that the first holder would be someone from philosophy or theology. Surely not an economist, I thought.

Then a few weeks later I received a second letter asking if we would not consider a Jesuit economist to whom I will just refer as Father H. He may well have been a great person but none of us in economics knew him or knew of his work. We were not even the slightest bit interested. "But," I said to my colleagues, "we can't just say no. We have to come up with someone else." Mike Mann and Joe Quinn both knew Bill Neenan and thought he would be great. We also had good reports on Bill through a fellow Jesuit and friend of Neenan named Bill Birdsall, who had been with us as a visitor.

I asked Mike to call him to see if he might be interested, and I followed up with a letter. Bill was a tenured professor at Michigan and was very happy there. But he was intrigued at the thought of a year or two in Boston and the more he learned of us the more interested he became. He came out to meet us in July 1978. In my file I have a copy of a bill from Legal Seafood for which I had requested reimbursement. Ten of us went to lunch and the total bill was $39.88, including the tip. I guess we didn't have much to drink.

Bill was by now very interested. He was committed to Michigan for the coming year but could arrange a leave for the following two years. Bill Neenan was awarded the first Gasson Chair and he arrived in 1979. Thus began a long love affair. Bill loved Boston College and we all loved him. He stayed on in the Gasson Chair for a second year and then in 1981 was named Dean of the College of Arts and Sciences. He then became academic vice president, and finally special assistant to the president. But to all of us he remained our friend Bill.

I remember introducing Bill at a function in which I said, "He's from Iowa, you know. You know where that is—just a notch below Minnesota." Bill responded at a subsequent time with, "Minnesota stands on the shoulders of Iowa."

Racism, Sexism and Affirmative Action

I wrote earlier about my involvement with the Black Studies Program and the Black Talent Program. The Kerner report issued in February 1968 laid bare the deep divisions in the U.S. along racial lines. There were stark differences in employment, education, housing, income, and wealth. Economists had for some years tried to explain the differences and had found that even after allowing for almost any measurable factor apart from race, Blacks fared less well than Whites. The only remaining variable that made any sense to most of us was racism.

We were aware of this as economists but it did not appear in the leading textbook, the one I was using, until the seventh edition that came out in 1970.[xxi] (The previous edition of this text was in 1967). This is just one small example of the change in racial awareness that was occurring at that time.

In the economist's model, discrimination based purely on race or sex should not persist. If Blacks with equal ability, education, and experience were paid less than Whites and had higher unemployment rates, then firms would hire the Blacks rather than the Whites, save some money, and make higher profits. The increase in demand for Black workers, as opposed to White, would eliminate the wage differentials.

But, we said, suppose the employers were racists. Then they would sacrifice something in profit to maintain their distance. But surely there would be some employers who would care more about profit than about maintaining distance. They would hire Blacks and would be the ones to thrive. The others would have to adapt or go out of business. Market forces should do the job.

But suppose most of the workers were racist. Then to employ Blacks in supervisory, or even comparable, positions would increase tension in the workplace and reduce productivity. So the employers would hesitate.

But then, said the economists' model, some firms would hire an all-Black labor force, enjoy lower costs, and earn higher profits. As economists we believed that the lure of money could certainly overcome a racial bias. Some firms would hire all Blacks at lower wages and make more money. Others would need to follow to stay competitive, and the differentials would be eliminated.

Okay, but suppose the customers were racist. Then they would think the product or the service of the all-Black firm would be less desirable and sales would suffer. It would be better to stay as one was. What came out of this analysis was the conclusion that if the entire society was racist then the disparities would not be eliminated by market forces. We would need to do something else.

I was teaching this by 1971 and had become convinced that the Kerner report was correct. We were a racist society and the attack on racism had to be at all levels. From my work with the Foundation for Brookline Housing I was convinced that the best hope would be through familiarity, through our children seeing Black children in our parks and playgrounds and then hopefully beginning to play with them. At Boston College this would mean recruiting Black students and Black faculty. Thus affirmative action was born.

Boston College launched its Black Talent Program in 1968 in an effort to bring in more Black students. Then to spur faculty recruitment of Blacks and women, we created the Affirmative Action Program in 1971. The women had awakened and said, "What about us? We are treated pretty shabbily too." Seavey Joyce had established COROW (Committee on the Role of Women at Boston College) in 1971 and it issued its report in 1972.

The report found that women on the faculty were paid less than men, even after allowing for differences in research output, quality of teaching, length of service, and reputation of the school from which they had a Ph.D. Women in the administration were far less likely to be promoted into supervisory positions, again allowing for length of service and qualifications. The research was done by a full professor in our economics department, Ann Friedlaender, and from my knowledge of Ann I could attest to the research being impeccable.

On seeing the report I took a look at the salaries in our own department and found that Ann herself was paid less than men of comparable qualifications. I was amazed and asked myself how this could have happened. In thinking about it I came up with two possibilities.

Ann had less bargaining power. She was married to an architect with a strong clientele in the Boston area and thus was less likely to come in with an offer from elsewhere. A second was that an administrator was always dealing with a limited pool for salary increments and might have seen her as not needing the money as much as a man who was the sole breadwinner of a family. Or the reason may have been something of which I am not aware. But the discrepancy was real.

The stated purpose of Affirmative Action at Boston College was to "provide equal opportunity in employment and education" but we understood that we very much wanted to increase the number of students who were Black, and later other minorities as well, and the number of faculty who were women or members of a minority group.

In terms of procedure we were to advertise positions that were to be filled and were to actively seek out women and minorities. We were to keep careful records of what we did and were to file an annual report. I crossed the t's and dotted the i's but had no success. When I began my term as chair we had two full professors who were women and when I finished in 1978 we had none. Alice Bourneuf had retired and Ann Friedlaender had been induced to return to the place of her doctorate, M.I.T. We had hired one person who was part Native American but one couldn't tell that by looking at him, so this didn't do much for us in terms of a visible presence. We had no other minorities on our economics faculty, either at the beginning of my term or at the end. Why not, one might ask?

In hiring in economics we reviewed the candidates and then ranked them. For each of them we also made a decision with respect to whether they were above the line (acceptable) or below the line (not acceptable). We then made an offer to the top-ranked candidate and if that was refused went on to the next one. If none of those above the line accepted an offer, we went back into the market or waited until the next year. We did decide that if a White male and a woman or a Black were of roughly equal rank, we would make the offer to the woman or the Black, but we found in every case that these candidates received offers from schools that outranked us.

In the early sixties McEwen and Bourneuf had achieved diversity by going for the best people they could get at a time when women, even though scarce at only 5% of the Ph.D.'s in economics, were not receiving many offers. Now, in the seventies, we were still going after the best people we could get but were finding that the women and the Black candidates (of which the percentage of Ph.D.'s was way below 5%) were accepting offers from schools that outranked us.

It occurred to me that in this competitive environment there were just three ways to achieve diversity. One, we could look hard for candidates that had a preference for Boston, and pursue them assiduously. This might work. It had been a factor in attracting Ann Friedlaender and only ceased to work when she got the offer from M.I.T. Two, we could decide to hire the best women or minorities we could get, even if "below the line." We rejected this approach as counterproductive, in that what we wanted was women and Blacks who would help to eradicate the stereotypes that were prevalent rather than reinforce them.

Three, we could focus on those Blacks or women who were above the line and give them offers that were too good to refuse in terms of salary, teaching load, and research assistance. I came to see this as the most promising approach but was not successful in making the case for it with our dean. My correspondence for the years 1971-78 has been lost, unfortunately, so I can't be sure I made the case in writing. (On completing my term as chair I had left my correspondence in the department filing cabinet, and then to my dismay it was discarded one spring in a massive cleanout of files.) But I do remember very clearly one time when at least verbally I presented such a case to our dean.

An outstanding Black student at M.I.T. was completing his Ph.D. and needed a bit of extra money for the following spring when he would be on the job market. I approached him about teaching a course for us in the spring and he would have come had I been able to give him a stipend that would have made it worth his while to come over here on two days of the week. I knew that our normal part-time stipend would not do the job and I urged the dean to let me offer an extra $1000, which in today's dollars would be an extra $4000. I was rebuffed, on the grounds of fairness to others, and I let it drop. Had he come, and liked it here, we might well have been able to induce him to come on full time. I fault myself for not having pushed the case harder, for this was exactly the kind of opportunity we needed to pursue.

We filled out the forms and recruited candidates, but to no avail. We just did not show the same imagination in thinking outside the box that A. Robert Phillips had shown in recruiting students for the Black Talent Program or that I had experienced in my work with the Foundation for Brookline Housing.

Economists believe in incentives. A congenial environment is clearly important, but a higher salary can make a difference as well. And perhaps a dean might have had one or two positions that could be given to a department as an extra slot for an outstanding Black or woman candidate. A department chair can be known to work wonders to get an additional slot.

Affirmative action at Boston College was far from successful, at least in Economics, either during my first term as chair, 1971-78 or in my second term, 1984-88. It may have been more successful in other departments, and in the administrative areas, but I don't have any data to determine whether that is the case. I just know it did not work in economics over that period of time.

Growing Pains in our Use of Language

One day in the mid-seventies a young woman showed up at my door and introduced herself as the editor of *The Heights*. We talked for a bit and then she asked if I might not begin using the term chairperson rather than chairman. I told her I found the term awkward but would begin to use it just as soon as *The Heights* began to use the term freshperson to refer to a first-year student. Yes, I was still a flippant young man.

And my comment wasn't quite fair. I had always thought of the term chairman as gender neutral, but in truth the term chairwoman had been around for a long time. And I had never heard the term freshwoman as an alternative to freshman. I was vaguely aware that the term chairperson was coming into usage as of the early seventies.

So the editor had a point. I wish at the time that either she or I had come up with the term "chair," which I would have been happy to use. It took until 1988 for Boston College to begin to use "chairperson" rather than "chairman" as a title for our department chairs. "Chairperson" continued to be used in the Boston College Bulletin as of my retirement in 2016, even with the much better term "chair" now widely used elsewhere. We still don't have a good alternative to "freshman." "First-year student" just doesn't quite cut it, at least to this observer.

The point of the above is that language does matter. It behooves us to make an effort to treat all people with dignity. But I would hope we might also be forgiving of those of us who continue to slip every once in a while. And I would hope, writing in the context of 2016, that we don't give up our commitment to the free exchange of ideas in our zeal to avoid giving offense.

In one of my first annual reports as chair of economics, I included the following, "We need one more man in the area of ..." Ann Friedlaender pointed out to me that I might have used "person" rather than "man," and I took this to heart. None of the men in my department picked up on the use of the phrase; nor did the deans who read the report. And none of us would have meant to exclude women in our search process. But that is where we were in terms of language.

A Black student came to my office one day to complain about a grade given him by one of our Teaching Fellows (advanced Ph.D. students who had full control of their courses). He was a campus leader and an outstanding young man. But I had reviewed the case and believed the grade to be justified. We talked for some time, getting nowhere, and we both dug in our heels, each of us convinced no doubt that we held the high ground. He finally said, "You wouldn't treat me like this if I were White," to which I responded, "Oh, come on. The conversation would have ended long ago if you were White." He followed up with "That's a racist thing to say," at which point I lost my temper. "Get out," I said. "The conversation is over."

I believed I had been bending over backward to hear him out, spending far more time on the case than was justified, and he believed he was being treated unfairly.

Al Folkard called me the next day to say that the student had come from my office to him, upset that he might have gone a bit too far. I told Al to tell him that I too might have gone a bit too far. We were all in the learning process. I didn't see the student again prior to graduation, but by twenty years later we were good friends. And we are good friends to this day. I do realize now that I missed a teaching moment—a chance to begin a meaningful conversation on racism, not just with this student but quite possibly with his broader circle of friends.

I noted earlier that in 1970, the strike semester, I had taught a course called Black Economic Development in the U.S., in which the students were solely from the Black Talent program. How did I achieve this? We simply didn't list the course among the course offerings until registration had been completed. In the next year I taught the course again, and this time it was listed and thus of necessity open to all students. I asked Julianne Malveau, an outstanding student recruited through the Black Talent Program, to teach it with me. She graciously accepted, and we worked well together. Julianne went on to get a Ph.D. in economics from M.I.T. and to have an outstanding career, culminating in a role as a college president.

Some years ago Julianne was invited to return to campus as the featured speaker for the Martin Luther King, Jr. dinner. After the talk she was to meet with the AHANA students at a reception in Hovey House, and some of the students asked me if I would like to come. I was quite sure I would be the only White person there, and I went with some trepidation. The students were as gracious as could be, but it did seem to me that I was restraining the party a bit, so I didn't stay long. I did come away with a better appreciation of what it must be like for a Black student to be alone in a sea of Whites.

The Budget Committee

One of the outcomes of the student strike in 1970 was an agreement to form a budget committee with student and faculty members along with key administrators. My colleague Frank McLaughlin served on the committee in its early years, and when my term as department chair ended in 1978 I ran for and was elected to the committee. I served from 1978 to 1982 and it was a fascinating experience.

The students saw their job on the committee as holding down the tuition increases to as little as possible, and the faculty representatives saw their job as getting as much as we could for faculty salaries. The administrators wanted to run a surplus so as to build up reserves and to undertake innovative projects. We had to at least balance the budget and it was difficult to do that, let alone provide for a surplus.

The officers of the university did not have to accept the recommendations of the budget committee, but they recognized that it would be good to have agreement on the major parameters of the budget from all members of the committee. That proved to be very, very difficult. But then in 1976 John Smith and Frank Campanella, working together, came up with the idea of depreciation-cost accounting.

Prior to this Boston College did not recognize depreciation on plant and equipment as a cost and I am quite sure that no university in the U.S. did so. We did allow for expenditures on maintenance, but college buildings were crumbling all over the nation due to deferred maintenance in the "stagflation" era of the seventies, when the U.S. had found itself in the grip of inflation and recession at the same time. Buildings needed major repairs and they needed modifications to deal with the surge in energy costs of the 1970s.

Why not, said Smith and Campanella, build in depreciation as a cost and then balance the budget with enough revenue to cover not only such cash expenses as salaries and utilities but this non-cash outlay as well? The funds would accumulate and be there when we needed them. Once depreciation was recognized as a cost, even though it was not an immediate cash outlay, a balanced budget could generate an increase in cash reserves.

Another innovation in finance that paid huge dividends over the years was the financing of new construction through HEFA. The Health and Education Financing Authority, or HEFA, had been created by the Massachusetts legislature in 1968 with important input from Charles Flaherty, a Boston College graduate and rising star in the legislature. Under HEFA, non-profits such as universities and hospitals, could borrow at the municipal bond rate, which due to tax advantages was a highly favorable interest rate.

John Smith seized on this and used HEFA effectively throughout the seventies and beyond. As alumni began to give once more through development campaigns, the funds raised were put into the endowment, yielding market returns, while the new buildings were financed with debt, much of it HEFA debt at a favorable interest rate.

The late seventies and early eighties were exciting years to be on the budget committee. Nothing was easy. Energy costs had exploded with the "oil shocks" of 1973 and 1979, and by December 1978 the inflation rate was 9% and rising. Boston College needed to determine its tuition rate and salary pool for the year to begin nine months hence and we had no idea whether inflation would be higher or lower by that time.

There was enormous pressure on government to do something but there was no real appetite for the wage and price controls we had experienced under Nixon in 1971-72. In September 1978 President Jimmy Carter announced we would have wage and price guidelines in an effort to control inflation and the guidelines were made explicit in December 1978. Price increases by any organization were to be limited to a half percentage point below their average for the years 1976 and 1977 and salaries (including fringe benefits) were to be increased by no more than 7%. For Boston College that would mean both tuition and salaries going up by no more than 7%.

The hope was that if most firms abided by the guidelines then both the prices people pay and the wages they received would go up at a lower rate than before and we would have brought inflation down with no one being worse off. The guidelines were announced as voluntary but with veiled and sometimes not so veiled threats of action against firms that did not comply. The president would "shame" any "irresponsible firm" that did not comply, and any firms with government contracts, or universities receiving federal aid, had to feel the pressure to comply.

I recall our discussion in the budget committee as clearly as if had been yesterday. The students argued that of course we must comply and hold down the tuition increase. The faculty representatives, including me, pointed out that if Boston College were to comply and others did not, then our faculty would suffer a serious cut in their real incomes (salaries adjusted for inflation), after having already taken a cut in the current year due to unexpectedly high inflation. I argued that the guidelines were unlikely to work and urged that we ignore them. I pushed for increases on the order of 11%, to make up for lost ground in the current year and keep up with inflation over the next, assuming inflation would stay at its current rate of 9%.

We settled on a 9.2% increase in tuition and an increase of 8.5% in salaries. Inflation over the next year turned out to be 13%, led by another spike in oil prices, so the guidelines clearly did not work. (In fairness, they had no real chance once the second oil shock hit in 1979.) For the following year, 1980-81, we increased tuition by 14% and salaries by 10%.

Over the first ten years of the Monan presidency, fall 1972 to fall 1982, the Boston College tuition rose at an average rate of 8.7% per year while inflation averaged 8.8% per year, and the average faculty salary rose at 7.4% per year. Salary increases for people in place did rise by a bit over 9.0% per year, so we didn't really lose ground to inflation. We just didn't move ahead, in real terms, at the rate we had all hoped to do. It was the average faculty salary that rose at the lower rate of 7.4%, since people who retired were replaced for the most part by beginners who commanded lower salaries. In terms of budget, this gap between tuition and the increase in average salary did provide funds for growth in areas outside the classroom. (The numbers given above are taken from tables I was updating on an annual basis for the budget committee over this period of time.)

It was only in later years that tuition, not only at Boston College but throughout higher education, began to rise much faster than did the cost of living, and salaries began to rise at least moderately faster. The first ten years of the Monan presidency were years of putting the house in order. They provided the basis for the immense growth that was to occur over the next 14 years.

A Diversion on Price Controls under Nixon

I noted that under Jimmy Carter there was no appetite for the kind of price controls we had under Nixon in 1971-73. Widespread controls inevitably produce distortions that make them unworkable for more than a year or two save in a time of major war as in World War II. I have to share just one incident of life under controls in 1971-73. I was chair of economics and arrived one morning in spring 1972 to find that our secretarial offices had been broken into. The only things missing were all four of our IBM Selectric Typewriters. The chairs, desks, and lamps were all in place.

In those days virtually all the typing was done by secretaries—we did not have desktop computers and most of us did not even have typewriters in our offices. Nearly all exams and handouts and correspondence went through our four secretaries. The typewriters would have to be replaced immediately and in this case I got quick assent from above. I called our supplier and asked how quickly they could deliver replacements, telling them just what we wanted. I was told, "Oh, we are out of those models." "What?, I responded. How can you not have them?" To which I was told, "We can give you an upgrade, a newer model." These would cost a bit more, but we could get them delivered by the next day.

I began to ask myself, "Why were those upgrades available but not the very popular Selectrics that we all loved?" And why were the typewriters stolen when nothing else was touched? The reason was that new products were exempt from price controls, since there was no base price from which to compute an increase.

By upgrading the Selectric, IBM had been able to claim it as a new product and escape the controls. Then, or so it appeared to me, they had slowed production of the old one, which was less profitable, in order to force buyers to take the new one. And the old model, being popular and in short supply, could be easily sold in the secondary market. And so they were stolen. This is just one small example of how efforts to control prices and wages lead to distortions that within a year or two lead to their removal.

The Flutie Years

Doug Flutie enrolled at Boston College in fall 1981. Boston College was the only school to recruit him and by the fifth game of his freshman year he was the starting quarterback. The Eagles lost that game, to Navy, but then went on to win four of the next six. Things were looking up. In 1982 Boston College finished 8-3-1, including a tie against Clemson, whose Tigers had been undefeated the prior year and had been voted number one in the nation. The Eagles went to the Tangerine Bowl, where they lost to 18th ranked Auburn.

They began the next year with a sold-out alumni stadium, but then they moved to Sullivan Stadium in Foxboro (the home of the New England Patriots) for the last two home games, against Penn State and Alabama. The Eagles won both of those, finished the regular season at 9-2, and went on to the Liberty Bowl, where they lost to Notre Dame by one point. They were ranked 13th in the nation going into the bowl game and finished 19th. Boston College football was back, in a big way.

In 1984 Boston College played all its home games in Sullivan Stadium. They finished the regular season at 9-2, with the only losses being to West Virginia by one point and to Penn State by seven points. They went to the Cotton Bowl, where they defeated Houston, and finished the season ranked number five in the nation. The wins included the famous "Miracle in Miami" and Flutie was awarded the Heisman Trophy.

Applications spiked with the Flutie years and this phenomenon, that of football performance having a positive impact on college applications, became known as the "Flutie Factor." Applications to BC were on the rise anyway, and there was some skepticism as to whether or how much this could be attributed to Doug Flutie. But subsequent studies, including one by our own Robert Murphy in Economics, did indicate a link between the football record and the change in number of applicants to a school.[xxii]

Sullivan Stadium was a difficult drive from Boston, and it is not likely I would have seen any of those games in 1984 but for BC's financial vice president and treasurer John Smith. John got a batch of tickets, rented buses, and invited faculty to come to the games with their spouses. He and his wife Helen rode those buses with the rest of us. We tailgated at Foxboro, got to see Flutie play, and had a terrific time. What John Smith did for faculty morale in that fall of 1984 went a long way to make up for the frustration over faculty salaries which by this time had not yet caught up.

The contribution of John Smith to Boston College over those years is not fully appreciated. He was an optimist, even in the darkest days; he was a financial genius, and he treated the faculty as though they were really something special. He also said whatever was on his mind at any time and that was refreshing, even though it was not what would now be considered politically correct.

Bill Doty and the Investment Club

I was sitting in my office one day early in fall 1982, when an economics major named Bill Doty came by and asked if we could talk. He wanted to start an investment club at Boston College, one that would deal with real money. He wanted students to learn about investing and was convinced they had to invest real money to do so. He had had some experience with managing virtual portfolios, as had I, and we both agreed that people tend to take much greater chances with Monopoly money than with their own.

Bill had approached the chair of the Finance Department, who was not sympathetic to the idea, and then he had gone to the chair of Economics, who sent him on to me. I told Bill that I shared his view that we need to invest real money in order to learn, but I could understand the skepticism he had encountered. I could see two serious problems. One, there might be a tendency for students to put in more money than they could afford to lose, and two, there would be the problem each spring of cashing out students who were about to graduate. Could we really be sure we had kept the records properly and that the departing members were getting back what they were entitled to?

I then told Bill that I had read about a club at another school that raised money from alumni and then managed it as a permanent fund. Bill thought that would be terrific. I told him to prepare a written proposal and then come back to me, thinking I would never see him again. That usually works.

Bill returned the next day with a written proposal that was very well done. I liked it and gave it just minor tweaking. And then I told him that there were some people he would have to talk to—Frank Campanella, our executive vice president, John Smith, our financial vice president, and perhaps someone in Development. He said fine, he would set up the appointments.

I immediately called Frank and told him a student would be coming to see him about an investment club. I said, "Now, don't just throw him out. He is an able kid and he has a pretty good idea." I did the same with John Smith. Frank liked the idea, as did John, and I gather they talked about it together. John Smith advised us not to go to Development, since they might not want us mucking around with alumni, asking for money.

Bill and I then got in touch with Student Affairs to get the club recognized, and we received wonderful support from Carole Wegman, who was Director of Student Programs.

Bill's father gave the first check, for $5000, to Fr. Monan during halftime of the Tangerine Bowl in December 1982, and we were well on the way. Bill got another $5000 apiece from two alumni whom he knew well and that $15,000 provided the basis for the portfolio. We did then get in touch with Development, with an arrangement under which the money would be given to Boston College, as a part of its endowment, but to be managed by the students in the investment club. This enabled us to use the University's Tax Identification number for the brokerage account and thereby to avoid a whole host of reporting issues we might otherwise have had to deal with.

The first investments by the club were in Seagate Technology, which did well, and in El Chico, a Mexican restaurant chain which did not do well. Bill, the first president of the club, and his vice president George had been to a Mexican restaurant to eat and they saw this as the future of dining. Following Peter Lynch's advice to buy what you know, they looked for a Mexican restaurant that was publicly traded and El Chico was the one they found. Of course not all Mexican restaurants are alike and it turned out that El Chico was not the wave of the future. But it was a learning experience.

Bill continued to contribute once he graduated and was active in the industry, and others gave as well. The students researched the stocks and made recommendations to buy or sell, which were then voted upon at a meeting. I went to the meetings and managed to bite my lip when I disagreed with a recommendation. From the beginning we wanted students to learn about investing and in that process we all make mistakes. And my own stock picks, for my own portfolio, hadn't done any better than those chosen by vote of the students. So who was I to give them advice on what to buy or sell?

The club did pretty well over the years, actually outperforming the market a bit, as measured by the S&P

500, and it is my best understanding that this has continued. I stayed with the club as its faculty advisor for 27 years, at which point it was time for me to move on. A large number of seniors have told me that in the job search when a recruiter saw Investment Club on the resume, that became the focus of the conversation. And if the student had made a stock recommendation at a meeting, that further moved things along. Bill provided a great service to Boston College students in founding the club, and I like to think I played a small part in it. Bill was recognized in spring 1984 as "the outstanding student leader" at the annual Leadership Awards banquet.

The Catholic and Jesuit Nature of Boston College

I mentioned earlier that when I told a friend I was coming to Boston College, he told me, "That's a Catholic school. You won't last a month at a place like that." My response was that I thought it would be interesting, and as it turned out I lasted 56 years.

In my first semester here I was profiled in *The Heights*. Some years later a student found a copy of the story and gave it me. Let me quote a few lines from it just to show what I was thinking as I came on the scene in 1960.

> I was very curious as to how a liberal arts
> education might differ in a Catholic school
> from a Protestant or nonsectarian school.
> There is a difference in that one is constantly
> aware of the religious heritage. I expected
> this, but I wondered whether there need be a

difference in the teaching of economics or the approach to truth in economic problems.

> I haven't seen any differences here. The appeal to knowledge as elsewhere in my experience is to all the wisdom of the ages. For a verification of our postulates, we look to what we can observe.

So if I found no difference in how I taught economics, and no one suggested that I should, then in what sense was Boston College Catholic? We began classes with prayer, the Jesuits were a visible presence in their clerical garb, and we required students to take far more courses in philosophy and theology than was the case at the average school in the U.S.

Most of the students were Catholic and they were expected to attend Mass, to make a three-day retreat sometime in the course of the year, and "to follow the Spiritual Exercises of St. Ignatius of Loyola." Non-Catholic students were exempted from the above and from the requirement to take theology courses.[xxiii]

New members of the faculty who were Catholic were expected to bring a letter from their parish priest. There were some books in the library that could only be read with special permission, and the Jesuit provincial might visit a class of a newly arrived faculty member. These things bothered me a bit but not enough to make me want to leave. I saw them as vestiges of the past (which they proved to be within five years) and the message I got from Walsh, Bourneuf, and McEwen was that Boston College was in the midst of rapid change.

The challenge, as the years went by, was how to become a leading national university, respected by its peers, and yet maintain what was distinctively Catholic and Jesuit at Boston College. By the late seventies and eighties the Jesuits were much less visible, both due to declining numbers and to most of them foregoing the collar, at least in the classroom and around the campus. We had reduced the requirements in philosophy and theology, and we increasingly both looked and felt like any other university. It became commonplace to say that B.C. stood for "Barely Catholic."

To many of our peers the term "Catholic University" was an oxymoron, or a contradiction in terms. Prospective hires did worry about what they saw as possible restrictions on academic freedom, and this had to be addressed. Department chairs started to take a short-cut approach, telling faculty candidates "Yes, Boston College is a Catholic school but don't worry about it. That won't impact you in your teaching or your research."

The leading Jesuits at Boston College began to sense that they were losing their school. In a quest for acceptance as a major university, we were losing the richness of the Ignatian tradition.

In June 1983 I received a letter from Joseph Duffy, S.J., the rector of the Jesuit Community. The letter was framed both as an invitation and a request for help. The Jesuits had been talking amongst themselves about the issues described above, but now they were reaching out to lay people at Boston College to join the conversation. The invitation was to spend a weekend at the Jesuit retreat house in Cohasset, as one of "about 25 faculty members and administrators, Jesuit and lay, to discuss their experiences, both positive and negative, of working in a university which identifies itself as Catholic and Jesuit."

I responded immediately that I would be delighted to come. By this time I had learned a bit about the history of the Jesuits, how in their early missionary work they had adapted to local customs and incorporated them into their worship. They had been ecumenical well before the term even occurred to the rest of us. In Latin America they had fought for the rights of indigenous people, to the great consternation of the colonialists, and their devotion to a sense of justice had led to suppression of the order for an extended period of time. I was aware of their leadership in higher education and also of their turn toward missions in response to the call of their Superior General, Pedro Arrupe, S.J., in 1975. I was eager to learn more.

The weekend was a great success. We had frank discussion and the lay people among us got a greater appreciation not only of what it might mean to be a Jesuit university when the number of Jesuits in residence was declining so rapidly, but also a deep sense of Ignatian spirituality. It occurred to me that perhaps the Jesuits were trying to enlist a number of us to carry on the tradition, and for me this was appealing.

I could not quite embrace the "Catholic" part of "Catholic and Jesuit"--my roots as a Protestant were too deep--but I was beginning to think of myself as Ignatian. The retreat was followed by a second in March 1986 and this one as well was immensely enriching. I was beginning to appreciate the extraordinary talents of Joseph Appleyard,

S.J., who was not only a great cook at the gatherings but was the most articulate person I had met in terms of the Ignatian tradition.

In the mid-eighties it even appeared that Boston College might no longer be able to refer to itself as a "Catholic" university. The pope, John Paul II, was giving serious consideration to a proposed regulation under which Church officials would examine and license theology professors at Catholic schools and might even declare that schools that did not meet standards were no longer Catholic. Our president, Fr. Monan, took strong objection to the proposal, but the newly installed Archbishop of Boston, Bernard Law, was very much in favor.

The Cardinal believed that he was in charge of everything Catholic in Boston and at a Boston College Commencement in 1986 he pretty much asserted that this was his school. There was a furor among the faculty who heard his remarks, and Fr. Monan found it necessary to make it clear to the Cardinal that Boston College was an independent university. It was issues like this that continued to make a good many faculty wary of the Catholic Church even as they revered the Jesuit order. Fr. Monan walked a tightrope as he continued to strengthen the university even as it had a rather chilly relationship with the Archdiocese of Boston.

Early in 1987 I was asked to attend a conference on American Catholic Higher Education to be held at DePaul University in April. The dates coincided with ones I had free during final exam period, so I jumped at the chance. Much of the discussion was focused on academic freedom, both concerning appearance on campus of speakers who opposed positions of the church, such as on abortion, and the then current discussion as to whether academic freedom was consistent with the screening of theology faculty by a group from Rome. There was also a good deal of discussion of whether being Catholic required a critical mass of faculty who were Catholic or at the very least were sympathetic to the mission of the Church.

It occurred to me that on sending me to the conference Boston College might see me as part of such a "critical mass" of sympathizers, but I just couldn't get that same warm and fuzzy feeling about "Catholic" as I could about "Jesuit" or "Ignatian." I still saw "Catholic" as authoritarian and "Jesuit" as open and inquiring. I saw the term "Ignatian" as deeply spiritual. I was serving a second term as chair of Economics by this time and in recruitment I had found Jesuit to be the stronger brand.

I knew of course that Jesuits were Catholics, but at the time it seemed as though the Jesuits were resisting the Catholics. The immediate issue of course was just resistance to one particular proposal from the Vatican, that of licensing theology professors, but this one went to the heart of academic freedom in the university. The Jesuits were seen as defenders against an assault by the Vatican, with Cardinal Law leading the Vatican charge right here in Boston, and J. Donald Monan, S.J., as the defender of the faith as we in academia saw it.

Over the prior twenty years I had developed an understanding of what it means in practice to be a Jesuit priest through a warm relationship with my colleague in Economics, Robert J. Cheney, S.J. Fr. Cheney was extraordinarily good with the students. He kept a big bowl of candy on his desk, which was just one factor that kept a steady stream of students coming in, he lived in a dorm as a visible presence there, he wore the collar, and he was faculty advisor to *The Heights* through its difficult times when they had been officially severed from the university due to the bugging of a trustee's meeting.   And he was clearly both a man of God and a man of this world.

In spring 1988 Bob Cheney told me he would like to nominate me for honorary membership in Alpha Sigma Nu, the Jesuit Honor Society.   I was deeply moved and accepted with great pleasure. That did it for me. By now I was practically a Jesuit, albeit still a Lutheran turned Episcopalian.

In September 1988 I received a letter from Fr. Monan inviting me to attend a conclave at Georgetown University in celebration of 200 years of Jesuit higher education in the United States.   It was called an Assembly of Jesuits in Higher Education and was sponsored by the ten Jesuit Provinces in the United States.   Each of the 28 Jesuit colleges or universities was given the prerogative of inviting a small number of lay colleagues to join the Jesuits and I was invited to be among the Boston College contingent.

This was right up my alley.   The group would be addressing problems common to all the Jesuit schools and the major themes I have addressed above concerning Boston College.   The speakers were to include the President of Cornell, the vice president of the National Conference of Catholic Bishops, and Peter-Hans Kolvenbach, S.J., who had succeeded Pedro Arrupe as Superior General of the Jesuit order. It was to be in June, so I would not have to miss any classes, and my expenses would be paid. So I was off again.

There was a realization throughout the Assembly that the Jesuits could not do it alone. We, their lay colleagues, would need to embrace the Jesuit vision and pass this along to our students. I returned to Boston College with a sense that I really was a part of the effort, with a sense of challenge and a sense of hope. While there I also gained a better understanding of Georgetown and of living near Washington, D.C. Sorry, Georgetown, that only enhanced my love of Boston and of Boston College.

In 1988 Boston College established the Jesuit Institute, through an endowment from the local Jesuit community, "to support the Jesuit, Catholic character of Boston College precisely as a university." The wording was important, at least to me, in that the primary emphasis was on "Jesuit," both in the title, in the placement of the words "Jesuit, Catholic," and in the term "precisely as a university." The institute was to promote seminars, research, and collaboration on matters at the intersection of faith and culture. I became a regular participant in one of the early seminars called "The Alienation of Intellectuals from Religion," led by a great Jesuit named Michael Buckley, S.J.

Participants in the seminar included Catholics, Protestants, Jews, and for a period of time a Muslim scholar. We read books such as one by George Marsden on how the Ivy schools had lost their religious identities,[xxiv] one by Richard Feynman on science and religion,[xxv] and parts of the Koran with the help of our Muslim brother. Out of the discussions came a growing consensus that one way for a Jesuit school to maintain its identity would be to embrace all the major faiths, to recognize that faith is an important part of the human experience, and to look at faith through the critical lens that academics can bring to bear.

As a result of this seminar, along with the retreats and conferences mentioned above, I came to realize that at Boston College I had a greater freedom than I would have found at an Ivy League school or a public university. I had the freedom to talk about matters of faith, and of God, in the classroom where appropriate and outside the classroom in seminars, lunches, or casual conversation. At an Ivy League school I would have been laughed out of the place for even entertaining such a thought, and at a state school I would have had to worry about the separation of church and state.

In 1998, to jump ahead just a bit, the Jesuit community provided a grant for the establishment of The Center for Ignatian Spirituality. Note here the term "Ignatian" in the title. "Wow," I thought, "this place is really coming around." I considered myself "Ignatian" by this time, and most of the students described themselves as spiritual but not religious. This center held great promise both for developing our spiritual lives and in terms of our brand in the recruitment of both students and faculty.

Then one day I heard Fr. Monan say, and I hope I am not doing him a disservice in paraphrasing him, "Anyone who pursues the truth with integrity, and who respects the dignity of every human being, is fully in accord with the Ignatian vision." That really sealed it for me.

A Greater Freedom

I said that when I came here I found that teaching economics was no different here than it had been at DePauw, at Brown, or at my first job in Ohio. But as the years went by my teaching did become different here in a way that I personally came to treasure. To me the spiritual aspect of life was in some mystical sense as real as the temporal, faith was an important part of what kept me going, and I had come to appreciate Ignatian spirituality.

It occurred to me that at an appropriate juncture I could bring this into the classroom. I was not required to do so but neither was I prevented from doing so. The milieu was such that it was okay, and I don't believe that would have been the case at either a state school or an Ivy League school.

So when I talked about economic growth and observed that creativity was the most important factor in growth, I would ask where creativity comes from. The Abrahamic tradition of Christianity, Judaism, and Islam is one of God as creator and human beings created in the image of God. That makes all of us creative. As children we are creative. Then, somehow, in all too many cases it gets dumbed out of us as we are forced to grow up. One need not believe in God to appreciate the virtue of creativity, and I was careful to point this out, but it is a possible basis for it.

In teaching my large section of Principles of Economics I dealt with forecasting. After pointing out that economic forecasting was about as good as weather forecasting—far from perfect but getting better—I asked the students who the world's first great forecaster was? Wasn't it Joseph, of Joseph and the Pharaoh, who successfully predicted seven good years and then seven bad years? Has anyone since had a record like that?

One year I wrote this down as a little poem, which I then began to share with the class. They seemed to like it, and they clamored for more. And perhaps they sensed a bit of creativity in what I was doing. The poem was intended not just to be an illustration of forecasting but also as a fable for our time.

Joseph and the Pharaoh

The pharaoh had this dream--
Seven really gorgeous fat cows
And seven lean and scrawny ones
And those mangy lean cows
Just took on and ate the fat ones.

Pharaoh woke with a start
The dream was so vivid.
"What does this mean? Who can tell me?"
For people believed in dreams in those days.
And none of his seers could tell him.

He fell asleep and had a second dream
This time seven ears of really good grain
And seven completely useless ones
And the bad ears destroyed the good ears
And still no one could explain the dream.

By now the pharaoh was really shook up
With two such similar dreams
And no one who could read them.
The "ears of grain" might have rung a bell
But all those smart people missed it.

And then his butler approached the pharaoh
The one he had put in prison and then let out
"There is this guy I met in the slammer
He is very good at dreams.
He got one of mine right on the money."

"So bring him to me," the pharaoh said.
And that was this young kid Joseph
So they pulled him out of prison,
Cleaned him up and brought him to court.
And the pharaoh asked, "Can you do dreams?"

And Joseph said to the pharaoh,
"I can't dig your dreams, but God can
And the big guy will give you an answer."
So the pharaoh told him the dreams
And Joseph gave him the answer.

"You are going to have seven terrific years
But then seven pretty rotten ones will follow
And if you squander the excess in good times
You will be in a sorry state when thing go bad
Your entire kingdom will be in the dust bin."

"So is this certain?" the pharaoh asked Joseph.
"You better believe it. Your dream was twofer.
That puts a fix on it." But there is still time.

God wants you to get your sorry ass in gear.
Get someone going to make the plans.

So the pharaoh pondered who to put in charge
His best and his brightest had let him down.
So he turned back to Joseph
The kid was bright, though a bit of a pain
And he did seem to have some channels open.

So the pharaoh put Joseph in charge
They built the granaries and waited.
The harvests came, the very best ever
And the people were set to indulge.
But Joseph said "No, store the excess."

The bins were bursting with plenty.
And the people were stirring and grumbling.
"What are we saving all this for?"
And Joseph said, "Tighten your belt."
"What? There is more than enough."

And the pharaoh even said to Joseph
"Might we give the people a feast,
Since the bins are bursting with food?"
But Joseph reminded the pharaoh
Of his dream and the days to come.

And the lean years came as foretold
With the heat and the sand and the dust
And the crops withered year after year.
But the food was there for the eating
And the kingdom weathered the storm.

And then one day when it was over
The pharaoh offered Joseph a beer
They talked about good times and bad
And the pharaoh said to Joseph,
"You know, Joseph, your God ain't so dumb."

So this Catholic school, at which I had worried from time to time about academic freedom, gave me a freedom that I might not have found in an Ivy or a state school. Rather than finding a limit on freedom of expression, I found an enhancement of it.

My Second Term as Chair.

Dick Tresch had succeeded me as chair of economics in 1978 and I had relocated from Carney to Lyons. Space was short in Carney, there was an empty office in Lyons, and it would not have been good to send a new person over there. So I went myself. Dick had a good run as chair and then Mike Mann took over in fall 1983. He had called me one morning in February 1984 to ask my advice and I had asked if I could call him back, since I had a student in the office. When I called back I got Helen, his secretary, who told me that Mike had collapsed in the mailroom.

I rushed on over and by that time the paramedics were there, trying to revive him. Mike had an arrhythmia, presumably controlled by medication, but his heart had skipped a beat and then stopped. The paramedics got it pumping again, but it was too late. Mike was in a coma and died about a year later without having awakened. A great colleague was lost much too young. Dick Tresch offered to take over for the balance of the academic year but he was due for a sabbatical the following year. I found myself being pressed to go back in as chair.

By this time I had started to do some consulting with attorneys as an expert witness. It was fun and it was lucrative and I knew I would have to cut back on it as a department chair, which tended to be a year-round job. Moreover, I hadn't really enjoyed being chair in my previous turn. I would come to work in the morning wondering what would go wrong and have to be fixed. I would find myself dealing with a problem and then rushing to class without having spent the half hour required to get my mind ready for class.

So I thought about whether I would be more miserable as chair myself or with an alternative candidate as chair, and I decided to go for it. But when I met with Deans Neenan and White to discuss it, I told them I didn't really need the job and to avoid a financial sacrifice I would need a $5000 jump in my salary. They said they would take care of me at increment time and I said, "No, you won't. At increment time I will be fighting for the rest of my department from a limited pool. I can't be bargaining for myself."

They said they couldn't do a salary adjustment now, so I got up to walk out. They called me back and said they would talk to Joe Fahey, the academic vice president. Joe went along with it and I breathed a sigh of relief. I was of course convinced that I wouldn't get another raise for quite a while, but when renewal letters came out in the spring there was another good increase. It seems the deans had rather liked my style, and they seemed to like what by now I was doing as chair.

This time I held the job for just four years. Near the end of my term we made three very strong appointments—Donald Cox, Peter Gottschalk, and Richard Arnott--who provided the impetus for a second surge of growth in the department. I am not sure we would have been able to get any of the three had Monan not been able to beat back what had been widely seen as an assault on academic freedom by Pope John Paul II and Cardinal Law of Boston.

It was our president, J. Donald Monan, S.J., with the support of the presidents of other U.S. Catholic colleges and universities, who brought to bear the most extraordinary diplomatic skills in saving the day. But it would take twenty years, in my view, to get back to where we were in dispelling the notion that "Catholic University" is an oxymoron.

The Bishops' Letter on the U.S. Economy

In November 1984 the U.S. Catholic Bishops released the first draft of a letter on the U.S. economy, entitled *Justice for All: Catholic Social Teaching and the U.S. Economy*. The letter was a clarion call to recognize the poor among us and to do something about it. It came as the U.S. economy was moving toward greater inequality, which was a reversal of nearly fifty years of lessening inequality from 1929 to 1976.

It came on the heels of an unemployment rate of 11.4% in 1983 (the highest in the past forty years), and a poverty rate of 15.2% in1983, which was the highest since 1965. Moreover it came out just two years after the election of

Ronald Reagan, at a time my friends on the left believed we were moving in the wrong direction.

The release of the letter was the cover story on major national magazines and it quickly became a topic of conversation on the T.V. talk shows. I read the letter and found parts of it clear and convincing, other parts wanting, but as a whole worthy of discussion. Moreover, it struck me as chair of the economics department in a leading Catholic university, that we had to take the letter seriously.

The letter asserted that the ratio of income in the highest quintile to that in the lowest was "unjust," to which my response was "What is the right ratio?" By January we co-sponsored a panel discussion with spirited but respectful dialogue on the issues raised in the letter. The panelists agreed on the goal of reducing poverty and inequality but differed on the role of government in achieving the objectives. We most particularly disagreed on the question of "economic rights" as asserted by the Bishops. Do we really have a right to "a job at adequate pay and self-realization in our work," and if so should we look to government to secure that right?

My colleagues carried the torch for an assertion of economic rights but I had some qualms. Let me briefly give my position as described in a story in *The Heights* on January 31, 1985.

> "I find the first part of the letter fair, clear and convincing," said Petersen. "It is a call to take care of the poor. It is a call to the country to recognize that we are all human beings."

However, Petersen said the letter raises many questions for him regarding the idea of economic rights. "Are these rights to be secured by the state?" he asked. "What is going to work well? To what degree and to what level and how far-reaching should the government's role be in solving these problems? I wonder if we haven't been learning that government can't solve all of our problems."

Yes, I was by this time a member of the Reagan revolution, but my concern with government granting economic rights went back to my high-school days, when our debate team went as far as the state tournament in arguing the welfare state (My position on the issue as of the mid-eighties is more fully stated in comments carried by *Boston College Magazine* in its summer 1987 issue.)

Over the next two years I appeared on panels at other schools in the area and spoke to such groups as the Boston Security Analysts Society and an assembly of social workers at the Massachusetts State House. More often than not I was the lone conservative voice, but that was all right. We had good discussions, spirited but congenial.

It struck me that to take the lead on discussion of the Bishops' letter, even as I differed with its policy recommendations, was an effective way to show what it means to be a Catholic and Jesuit university. In retrospect, I take some pride in what we did.

Work as an Expert Witness

In 1979, following a seven-year term as department chair, I was looking for things to do. I was asked to comment on a paper to be given at an economics meeting in Boston on the Small Loans industry. A young attorney in the audience asked me following the session whether I might like to do some work for them. Interest rates on loans were regulated and the lenders were asking for rate relief from the regulatory commission.

I was given financial reports for the leading firms and did an extensive study of their revenues and costs. The costs of doing business had risen substantially with the inflation of the seventies, but the interest rates the firms could charge had not changed. I found that the firms were not earning competitive returns and testified to that effect. The firms did get rate relief, the attorneys were happy with my work, and my career as an expert witness was launched. I began to get calls from other attorneys.

Most legal cases are settled out of court or they take years for a trial to take place. The first one in which I was scheduled to testify in court came to trial in March 1981. I discovered that the question of whether one is an "expert" is a rather curious one. Once you have been recognized in court as an expert, you tend to be so recognized by other courts. But if you have not testified in court you are not routinely accepted. The opposing attorney in this case moved to have me disqualified on the grounds I was not an expert and he tried to show this by going through my resume.

My resume was sparse, as you can well imagine from what I said earlier concerning my failure to publish. In going through it, the attorney noted a piece I had published, and then asked, "And that was just two pages?" "Yes," I responded. And then he said, "This other piece, that was just four pages?" with the emphasis on "four." This time I answered, "I really don't remember how many pages it was." He came right back with, "It says right here on your resume, pages 2-6," to which I responded, "I believe that is five pages, sir." The judge went with his fingers, 2, 3, 4, 5, 6, and said, "That's right, five pages." The attorney was a bit flustered and I was accepted as an expert.

Why did that come to me so quickly? Was it because I was smart? No, I had been teaching econometrics and had corrected a common error just about a week before. If we have a data set with numbers from 1960 to 1970, how many observations do we have? We have eleven, not ten. Sometimes we get lucky. And sometimes when we try something new, even just a new course such as econometrics was to me, we get rewarded in a way we cannot anticipate.

In that very first trial, my testimony was not quite completed when it was time to adjourn for the day. The judge asked me if I could possibly come back the next day. In a moment of weakness I said yes, perhaps because the judge had been kind to me and perhaps because I realized that the team I was working for would rather not give the opposition an extra day to regroup. But this was a problem. I had a class scheduled for that day and would need to cancel it.

I had already missed four classes at Boston College, one in 1970 during the tuition strike when I forgot to go, and three in 1979 when I had been sent to San Francisco on university business and an airline strike prevented me from getting back on time. I did not want to miss another one and in this case I would have a moral dilemma. I would be paid for testifying and I would be paid for the class I was scheduled to teach at Boston College.

I cancelled the class but did so with a certain sense of guilt. In the very next class, I told the students where I had been and even the little story about the five pages. I also told them how a math teacher had years earlier explained what an expert was. He wrote on the blackboard, "x = unknown." And then beneath this he wrote "a spurt is a drip under pressure." Then I told them I was being paid to testify, about $200 for that day, and I would like their thoughts on what we might do with the money. Some of them said, "Keep it," and I was hoping for the University Chorale, which was raising money for a trip to Rome. The class decided to give it to Oxfam America, which was fine. I sent the check, and of course for the next ten years I got annual solicitations from the organization.

The definition from my Prof. Arnold, that an expert is an unknown drip under pressure, paid dividends for me over the years. It kept me grounded and this made me a more effective witness. I enjoyed the testimony, even cross examination, and at times experienced what the psychologist Mihaly Csikszentmihalyi refers to as "flow," or athletes refer to as "in the zone." I had found something I was really quite good at, and the calls kept coming. I testified another 35 times over the next 34 years but did not miss another class due to a court appearance.

I did miss two more classes in 2015, when a brother-in-law's funeral was scheduled for a weekday rather than a weekend. I thus broke a streak of over 30 years without missing a class and this did not go down easily. My mother's funeral, my father's funeral, and my sister's funeral had all been held on weekends and I didn't see why this one had to be on a weekday. Oh well, every streak has to end.

In my second court appearance I believe we broke new ground in terms of precedent. (You can read about this if you like by searching "Harold Petersen Donahue v. Draper.") I only mention this to indicate that I had found something I was good at, and this gave an enormous boost to my confidence. I knew I had arrived when in 1994 a classified ad appeared in *Lawyers Journal* looking for copies of reports or depositions of Harold Petersen.[xxvi] Someone was looking for inconsistencies in my work in an effort to exploit them.

In 1988 I was hired by the defense in the Eugene Doran case. Doran was a highly successful real estate agent who was sitting in a barber chair getting a haircut. A contractor was working behind a thin wall with a nail gun and a nail came through, lodged in Doran, and left him a quadriplegic. Doran assembled a term of lawyers to bring suit against the contractor, the hardware store at which he had rented the nail gun, and of course the nail gun's manufacturer, the one with deep pockets, Stanley Tools.

Doran's earnings had been in the mid six figures, and a plaintiff economist had estimated the economic loss at about $12 million, by projecting future earnings and then discounting back to present at a discount rate of 2%. The discount rate is there to allow for the fact that if you get a settlement you can earn interest on it, and thus you don't need quite $1 million to replace $100,000 per year for ten years. The lower the interest rate, the less you can earn on money received now, and thus the greater the loss. Plaintiff attorneys loved a low discount rate, and the judge in the case was Judge Tauro, who was known at the time as "two-percent Tauro."

I was prepared to argue that the earnings in question were those of a business and should be valued as we value a business, with an appropriate multiple to earnings. This would still lead to a sizeable loss, one of about $6 million. The case did not go to trial. The defense did not want the jury to see Doran sitting there in his wheelchair, a person who got paralyzed while getting a haircut, and the defense attorneys knew they were up against two-percent Tauro.

So the parties settled for an award of $15.3 million. I happened to be watching TV when the decision came on the news and Doran appeared on the screen with a reporter. He was asked, "Mr. Doran, what are your plans now?" to which he replied, "I look forward to going back to work." It had not occurred to any of us that his mind was fine and he could go back to work. So little do we appreciate what those we call disabled are in fact able to do. But he clearly deserved the award, perhaps not in terms of economic loss, but in terms what that nail had done to his life. So I had no regrets.

I realized at some point that consulting did put me in the midst of another moral dilemma. It was not the time I devoted to it. I always worked 60 hours per week and

Boston College got a good 50 of those hours. And I was convinced that the work with attorneys enhanced my teaching, both in term of course content and because of the confidence it gave me.

But I was using university resources in terms of the library, the office, the computer, and paper. I knew I should be paying for this but didn't want to keep track of every little item and then mail checks to the treasurer's office. And they wouldn't have known how to handle them, anyway, in an accounting sense. So I decided simply that 10% of my consulting income would go back to Boston College, half of that directly in a check each year to the development office, and half to be kept in an account I would administer myself.

This meant that not only was I was impressing Development as a big giver, but I also had a separate fund which I could spend as I chose. I gave a $20 bill to nearly every student group in McElroy that was raising money, I bought books for students who couldn't afford them, and I helped sponsor a favorite student in Teach for America. I was having a ball, but my approach was a bit unorthodox. So I ran it by our Dean, Bill Neenan, who told me it was a splendid approach. I called it the "Harold Covers his Ass Fund." (Don't ask me for money now—the balance is down to virtually zero.)

Following September 11, a group of attorneys called Trial Lawyers Care was formed to provide pro bono assistance to the families of the victims. They recruited economists to do reports on the lost income to survivors, also pro bono, and I was asked if I would do one or two. I said of course I would—we all wanted to do what we could--and two reports led to three, and then four, and finally to eleven reports. I met the special moderator Kenneth Feinberg at a hearing on a case and was able to appreciate the sensitivity with which he dealt with the families.[xxvii] I received a letter of thanks from a young widow and mother and marveled how she could write this after what she had gone through. All I had done was to write a report.

I could go on for another thirty pages on some of the legal cases, but this is enough to make a point. I include it to illustrate how activities beyond the classroom can enhance those within it, and that to stay fresh as a classroom teacher for 56 years, one needs to be involved out there in the world beyond.

Fr. Woods and the Evening College

James A. Woods, S.J., became Dean of the Evening College in 1968, and I was teaching for him either from that date onward or very shortly thereafter. Fr. Woods was there for me when I needed extra money, and I continued to stay with him when I no longer needed the money but believed in what he was doing.

As Boston College became more selective throughout the eighties and nineties, more and more of the students came from wealthy suburban families. They were good students and I enjoyed working with them, but their accustomed life style was clearly a cut above my own. The students in the Evening College reminded me of those first-generation day students of the sixties, many of whom were working all night to raise the money to pay the tuition and then coming to class during the day. They had an incredible work ethic and a great desire to succeed.

In the Evening College it was possible for anyone to come. Standards were high, but no one was denied a chance, and a degree could be attained at a reasonable cost. To me there was something very appealing about that. If you asked Fr. Woods how he was, the answer was always the same, "Couldn't be better." His door was always open to the students and to me. I only stopped teaching in the Evening College when I could no longer teach for three hours at night and still be fresh the next day.

There was one little item on which a number of faculty members caused Fr. Woods some consternation. The students in the Evening College were required to take thirty courses for the degree, which meant that by taking two courses per semester and two over the summer a student could graduate in five years. This was feasible but to require more would have been a stretch.

But the day-school students were required to take thirty-eight courses, and they got essentially the same degree. When a number of us asked whether this was reasonable, to give the same Bachelor's degree for 30 courses in one school while requiring 38 in another, Fr. Woods promptly made his courses four-credit rather than three. He now said that his degree required 120 credits whereas the day-school degree required only 114.

When I pointed out that I teach exactly the same course in the Evening College as I do in the day school, he had an easy answer. "Oh, but these students bring their work experience to bear. That makes the courses more valuable." Case closed. I had to admire him. Here was one more savvy Jesuit who knew how to get things done. He cared about the students and he had a good sense of how much he could require without making the quest seem unattainable.

In 1993 Fr. Woods celebrated his 25 years as Dean by putting together a book of reflections by faculty who had been with him over that entire period of time. He asked me to submit a chapter and when I didn't get the copy to him on time he wrote it himself and put my name on it. He shared the copy with me just before the book was about to go to press. What he said of me in the lead-in to the chapter was highly complimentary, and what he said in the text was all right, but it wasn't me. It surely wasn't my writing style and it wasn't quite what I would have written. (You can check out the book. It is called *Opportunities*.)

When I told him that he couldn't put something in with my name on it that I hadn't written, his response was, "You did write it. What is there is all of the things you have said to me in the office over the years. I just wrote it down for you." I should have been grateful, given how sparse was my record of publication. Oh, I have to admire the man.

Fr. Woods had honored me by awarding me the Loyola Medal just the year before. He had every right to expect that I would write something for his book and get it to him on time. I took it as a lesson not to procrastinate.

In 2004 Fr. Woods published a second book, this one called *Expectations*. He included a chapter that "blends the thoughts" of five professors, including me. I appreciated the subtle difference and didn't mind my name being there on the cover along with that of Fr. Woods and 11 others.

Don't misunderstand me in my recounting some differences with Fr. Woods. I so much admire that outstanding Jesuit for what he did for all those students and what he did for me. He was right when he wrote in that book, *Expectations*, "the carryover from teaching in the Woods College provides a perspective which inexperienced students cannot impart, thus enriching daytime classes more than would have been possible otherwise." I treasure the Loyola Medal as given me by Fr. Woods and I value him both as a mentor and a friend.

Advisor to Five Student Groups

I spoke earlier of the Boston College Investment Club, to which I was faculty advisor for 27 years. But there were other student groups as well with which I became involved. In the early eighties the College Republicans asked me if I would be their advisor. They had heard me debate on behalf of Ronald Reagan and liked what I had to say. The people in student affairs were delighted to have me take on the job, since the College Republicans had been a thorn in their side for some time. Student Affairs hoped that someone just might get them to behave. My goal was for them to advocate strongly but to be civil, even to the Democrats, and to have elections in their own club which were fair and transparent.

We got along pretty well, and when in 1989 I decided to run for Town Meeting in Brookline I asked some of them if they would like to get involved in a local election, just for the experience. The elections in Brookline were hotly contested at the time, with rent control the big issue. Rent control had been fine with Brookline voters until a controversial court decision had forced a cut in taxes on rent-controlled properties and a consequent jump in taxes on homeowners. Rent control did not look nearly so good to those liberals in Brookline once it was costing them serious money. It was just possible that a conservative, even a Reagan supporter, might win in Brookline.

I ran a pretty good campaign, if I do say so, and on election day had two lovely young coeds standing at the polls handing out cards urging a vote for Petersen. I won, beating out a highly respected incumbent, and one of the losing candidates (not the incumbent) was an instructor in our History Department at Boston College. I had noticed on election day that he was not happy to see the students at the polling place.

Now he charged that I had pressured my students into working on my campaign, with the implication that to refuse might impact their grades. The students involved were in fact not any I had in class but were eager volunteers. I made this clear to my colleague and a possible scandal was short lived. The College Republicans were delighted to have played a part in a winning campaign and in the contentious atmosphere that followed, even if for just a short period of time. I had fun working with them over the next ten years.

Shortly after I took up with the College Republicans, a new group, The Conservative Forum, asked me to be their advisor. This was a group of students who wanted debates and discussions that would be sure to include the conservative point of view, so it was another natural for me. I was eager to have such discussions and I could be the conservative speaker if there was no one else to do so.

By 1987 I found that somehow I was the faculty advisor to five student groups, having added the Economics Association and Omicron Delta Epsilon (the Economics Honors Society) to my portfolio. (I was still with the Investment Club as well, attending their meetings on a weekly basis.) The Dean of Student Affairs, Robert Sherwood, had become a close friend through my interactions with his office, and in spring 1988 he nominated me for the Rev John R. Traska, S.J., Award for mentoring in extracurricular activities.

His nomination prevailed with the awards committee, and in accepting the award I did point out that Bob and I were buddies. I thought at the time that the award was given to me just for having been advisor to five clubs, but on reflection think it might have been for a bit more than that. I did believe in life outside the classroom.

I knew that my teaching was enriched by working with the student clubs, even as it was from being active in my church, my town, and my consulting business. So it would be natural for me to believe that many students might do better in their classes if they were also involved in the world around them. Fr. Traska, in whose name the award was given, had clearly believed that, and he was one more in that long line of Jesuits who had done so much to make Boston College what it was. So I was deeply moved to be given an award to which his name was attached.

Teaching and Doing in the Field of Investments

My interest in the stock market began with placing bets at the track as a graduate student at Brown and then with a summer fellowship to Wall Street in 1956. My Ph.D. thesis dealt with risk and how a firm raises money. And from about 1961 onward I taught a course in capital markets—stocks and bonds—nearly every year over the next fifty-five.

I had taught in the field of investments but hadn't done any investing until about 1966. Then I took the plunge. I borrowed some money against my life insurance and bought two stocks. (I am not recommending this for you. I just had to get in the game if I was going to teach it.) One of the stocks did all right and the other not so well. Then I tried mutual funds, buying the ones that had been doing well. From this I learned that past success is no predictor of future success, and about the same time I discovered that there were academic studies bearing this out.

This took me back to my childhood days at the Polk County Fair in Fertile. I would be betting on whether the ball would settle in the green cup. If it had been landing green for a while I would bet against green on the grounds that surely things would have to even out. Or I would bet green on the grounds that green was on a roll. In fact the ball had no memory of where it had landed on the previous rolls. And the stock market is like that. Future returns are almost completely independent of past returns. This holds for particular stocks and for a broad index of stocks.

Academics refer to this as the efficient market hypothesis. Stock prices do move with new information—up on good news and down on bad news—but when there is new information the price responds immediately. Let's suppose firm XYZ develops a new drug that makes the stock of the firm worth $40 rather than its current $20. A lot of people with big money at stake realize this and act very fast. We find a good many buyers but very few sellers at any price below $40 and the price immediately moves to $40. Those who were lucky enough to be holding the stock at $20 double their money but no one else gains from the news.

The implication of the above is that one cannot beat the market except by chance or by the use of inside information, and there is a risk of jail time in using inside information. Most us who are academics in finance believe that the evidence is pretty strong in favor of efficient markets, but as practitioners we keep trying to beat the market. And why not? The bad news is that we can't beat the market except by good luck, but the good news is that we can't do worse than the market except by bad luck. So why not have fun trying?

In 1976 my youngest daughter came home from school one day and told me about an interesting exercise. The teacher had asked the students what they want to do when they grow up and she had said, "I think I want to be president of IBM." "Really," I responded, and "What did the teacher say?'" "She asked me why, and I said I kind of think computers are the coming thing."

Wow. I was impressed, and I followed this up by reading the stock pages with her and most particularly any stories about IBM. Then I decided that if she wanted to be president she should start by being a stockholder. Christmas was approaching and so I called my broker and said I wanted to buy 10 shares of IBM for my daughter. How terrific, I was thinking--a good investment and also a Christmas present.

We reinvested the dividends, along with the initial shares, and by the time she was a senior in high school the holding had grown substantially. Then she said one day, "Dad, I think we should sell IBM." "No," I said, "It's great stock. Hold onto it." This was in 1988, when IBM was near a peak which wouldn't be reached again for 12 years. We finally sold it in 1994 when she needed the money for a down payment on a condo, and I made up the amount we had lost by hanging onto it. She could have become a good stock analyst, if not president of IBM, but she became a social worker instead. She is great at what she does.

By the early nineties most of my wealth was in my house—paying down the mortgage as the house rose in value—and in my retirement fund, TIAA-CREF. Boston College had a generous match and I put the maximum into the fund. Initially we had just two choices, a bond fund and a stock fund. I could choose how much to put into stocks but had no discretion beyond that. What fun was that for a frustrated academic who wanted some action in the market?

Academics in investments and finance dream of finding a market inefficiency—a stock or a sector that is so underpriced that a gain looks almost certain. They are hard to find—they are like $20 bills lying on the street. They are much less likely to get dropped than pennies and when they do get dropped they get picked up right away. In the mid-nineties I found an inefficiency that looked as though it had potential.

CREF had added a money market fund, an equity index fund that was all U.S., and a global stock fund that was about half U.S., about 40% European, and about 10% Pacific. CREF had no transactions fees for switching back and forth and provided a toll-free telephone number for placing orders. (This soon became an online transaction rather than a telephone one.) As with most mutual funds, securities were priced each day at their value as of the closing of the New York Stock Exchange, 4:00 p.m. Eastern Time. Any order placed during the day was executed at that closing price.

I wondered how CREF could price the European and Pacific stocks as of 4:00 New York time, when those markets would have been closed for some hours. I learned that the foreign stocks were priced as of the closing of their own markets. This meant that if some good news developed in the afternoon of New York time, and this was news that would be good for stocks worldwide, that the European and Pacific stocks could be bought for less than they were worth. The good news would be reflected in their prices on the following day.

I began to track the daily price changes of the U.S. fund and of the global fund. I discovered that when the U.S. fund went up (or down) by at least 1% on a day, chances were better than 2 to 1 that the global fund would tend to go up (or down) on the next day. I had tracked the data for 1996 and then in 1997 began to act upon it. If I was in the office about 3:30 p.m. I would turn on the computer and check the stock market.

If the U.S. market was up by at least 1% for the day, I would buy global and reverse the trade the next day. There was some risk of course. We could have bad news overnight, global would take a beating the next day, and I would lose on the trade. But I won more than I lost, about 2 to 1, and CREF would mail me confirmations of every transaction.

I was making some money, and I was excited at having found a market inefficiency, but I also realized that this really wasn't good for my colleagues in CREF, even if it only cost any one of them less than a penny a year. Once again, the moral qualms began to get to me. So I wrote to CREF, explained what I had found, and urged that they do something to correct the mispricing of foreign securities.

CREF responded that they were aware of the problem and that "one solution would be limit the frequency of timing of inter-fund transfers, or to impose a charge on them. We have so far been reluctant to limit the freedom of CREF participants to move between accounts, particularly when the practice is extremely limited."

I shared my correspondence with my colleagues in economics out of the belief that the best way to get CREF to respond would be to get more people in the game, but I am not aware that anyone close to me followed my lead. Others in the CREF family did catch on, however, and within another year the practice was no longer "extremely limited." Now CREF did respond by limiting the number of transfers into and out of the global fund. Later they adopted what came to be known as "fair value" pricing, in which they used information from futures markets to better price the foreign securities as of 4:00 p.m.

So the ball game was over, but it was fun while it lasted. The most I lost on any one day was $12,000 and the most I gained was about $20,000. Not bad for a few minutes each day. Over the two-year period I added an extra 10% to the value of my retirement fund.

The Masterworks Group

In 1992 a group of faculty led by David Lowenthal and Ernest Fortin, with the enthusiastic support of our Dean Robert Barth, S.J., put together a "Masterwork Study Group," which soon came to be known simply as the Masterworks Group. The plan was to meet occasionally for dinner at 6:00 p.m. and then have a leisurely discussion of a classical work of literature, poetry, or art. The meetings would be three or four times a semester and would be in Connolly House[xxviii] if that venue was available.

I couldn't make the meetings that first year, since I had an evening class on the night of the week that worked best for most people. But for the following year I adjusted my schedule so as to be sure I could make the meetings, and I have been a regular in the group since that time.

Our readings ranged from Plato to Shakespeare, to Aristophanes, to Melville, to books of the Old and New Testaments, to poetry of Yeats and of Stevens, to art work of Rembrandt and of Durer, to Hawthorne, to Dante, and to many more. To me this was the classical education that I had missed as an undergraduate, and I loved it. Too much of our time as academics was spent in busywork and in our disciplines. The Masterworks evenings were what we had dreamed academic life would be like but had not found to be the case.

One evening early on, when we were discussing what to read next, I said, "I've never read *The Republic*. Can we do that?" The others said it would be an admirable choice. And then a week later David, our leader, called me to ask me to lead the discussion. David Lowenthal, Ernie Fortin, and Mark O'Connor had studied *The Republic* for years, and I hadn't even read it. Whatever would I do?

I was nervous but knew I would be among friends. So I spent some time with *The Republic* and came up with a couple of ideas. I started by asking whether the U.S. government was more a republic or a democracy as Plato used the terms. I held out for "republic" in that we were ruled by philosopher kings who just happened to be dead. Our constitution, as bequeathed to us by our founding fathers, was the ultimate arbiter of whether something was lawful or not.

And then I asked whether Plato's Republic might be a model for corporate governance. Might our system work better if we had a few more "philosopher kings" on our Boards of Directors? So it went all right. My learned colleagues were most kind to me, and I began to believe that perhaps I could do something across disciplinary lines. When I finally began to teach in the Capstone program in 1999 I included Plato's Republic on my syllabus and posed the same questions to my students as I had to my Masterworks colleagues. The Masterworks experience turned out to be one more of the jewels I take with me from my years at Boston College.

Capstone

In 1990 Dean Robert Barth, S.J., convened a meeting of a small group of faculty to talk about a special, interdisciplinary course for seniors in which they would reflect on where they have been and where they want to go. The idea had come from two of my good friends in the theology department, James Weiss and John McDargh, and James Weiss was named the director of the program when it was launched the following year.

I was part of the discussion, and was intrigued, but at the time was terrified at the thought of teaching an interdisciplinary course. The Capstone courses were to deal with four topics: 1) work or career, 2) family or relationships, 3) religion or spirituality, and 4) civic involvement or community. Students were to be encouraged to take a close look at their lives to date—courses taken, activities, faith experience—and then to think about the kind of life they hoped to lead.

It struck me that this kind of course went to the heart of what I had come to understand as the essence of Ignatian spirituality: be attentive, be reflective, and be loving. I am sure Fr. Barth saw it the same way and I was delighted that he had been so supportive when James Weiss approached him about the program. Jim asked me to teach in the program but I couldn't imagine myself teaching topics that cut across theology, sociology, philosophy, psychology, and political science. What did I know about these fields?

Jim kept after me and at last, in October 1998, I gave him a proposal for a course. I would call it Business as a

Calling, after a book I had used by Michael Novak.[xxix] Novak was a theologian who wrote about business and economics, and I had used his book in my large section of Principles of Economics. It worked well there, so why not in a Capstone Course? Moreover, I was 65 years old by this time and so if not now, when?

I had come to be a passable teacher in classes with a lecture format but had no experience in teaching a small seminar. I did know from my other classes that it was difficult to get the students involved in discussions. So I decided that I would do the first two classes in my Capstone course and from that point on the students would take turns in leading the discussion. It worked well. I found that when students led the discussion, the others students were much more likely to respond and even to engage in a conversation.

I learned to bite my lip from time to time, since if I jumped in too quickly to correct what I saw as an error, the conversation would grind to a halt. It turned out to be so much better with all of us learning together than with an "expert" speaking the "truth" and students just writing it down.

The students loved the course and so did I. I will never forget a student telling me that this was the first time she had made a presentation to others. (This was a senior at Boston College.) She had been terrified but then felt so good when she found she could do it.

Capstone and Life as a Journey

The Capstone course was of great value to me, and I believe to my students as well, in beginning to understand what it means to view life as a journey. We began the course as one of vocational discernment. Do we all have a calling, something we are meant to do quite apart from the money it might provide? If so, how might we best discern what that calling might be? Does the question of calling go beyond what we might think of as vocation in terms of the clergy, or possibly teaching or nursing? Might even business be a calling?

I hadn't thought much about this question as I went through college. To me the objective was to be able to get a job and earn a living. I was fortunate to be able to take a detour through graduate school and then land a job in a university, which job for all its frustrations was a pretty good one. But for me to even ask whether this was what I was meant to do was a stretch.

Not so for students at Boston College in early 2000s. By this time they had all been exposed to the "Three Key "Questions" as posed by the beloved theology professor Michael Himes. "What are you good at? What brings you joy? What does the world need you to be?" They were thinking about discernment and were wondering whether indeed there might be something they might be called to do. And if so, how in the world might they find out just what that might be?

We used a number of books in the Capstone course, but four of them stood out as favorites over the years. The first of these was the aforementioned book by Michael Novak, *Business as a Calling: Work and the Examined Life*. This one made the case that business can indeed be a noble profession, and even a calling, as can virtually any profession. A second was a short novel, *The Alchemist*, by Paulo Coelho. This one follows a young man who leaves home to pursue his dream, which he has been persuaded must take him to the pyramids of Egypt. He loses all his money on the way and needs to stop, take a job, and regroup. Through Coelho we see that there may be circumstances in which we have to postpone the dream, as life intervenes, but that it can at one point be resumed. What counts is how we react to what life throws at us.

A third favorite book was *What are We?* or what we called the little red book. It was written for freshmen at Boston College, and it does not list an author as such. (I suspect that Joseph Appleyard played a major role in putting it together.) This one deals with Ignatius of Loyola, with Ignatian spirituality, and with the history of Boston College. Through the journey of Ignatius, that of the Jesuit order, and that of Boston College, we begin to see that we are all on a journey.

Finally, a book by Bill Strickland, *Make the Impossible Possible*, once it came out in 2008, became a huge favorite of the class. This one shows the immense potential that is there in every human being, just waiting to be unleashed. (I will say more about Strickland a bit later.)

What begins as a course in how we might best choose a vocation or a profession moves by the end of the course to a realization that what might be most important is how we live our lives.

Capstone and the Closet Feminist

I taught the course each spring from 2000 through 2006 and then decided to take a break from Capstone in spring 2007. By February I realized how much I was missing the course. Then I got a call from Jim Weiss telling me that Sr. Mary Daniel had become ill and he was looking for someone to fill in until she could return. I asked Jim to let me do it—I was missing Capstone.

Mary Daniel O'Keefe, O.D., was an associate dean and a devout Catholic. But when I took on her course and looked at the readings, I discovered she was also a feminist. Perhaps the term is not quite accurate. But through her reading list I did encounter for the first time those parts of the book of Wisdom that saw "Wisdom" as feminine and as coming from God. I learned that Sophia was the goddess of wisdom in Greek mythology and that a good case could be made that if we were to think of two aspects of the trinity in masculine terms (father and son) then we might well view the Holy Spirit as feminine.

Mary Daniel's illness lingered and so I met with the class over a period of some weeks. She wanted to share her stipend for the course and I had to tell her "No way! Where I came from when a farmer got sick the other farmers came in to do the plowing and the planting. And they wouldn't take a nickel for it." She relented but did have her sister go out and buy gifts for me.

Mary Daniel came back for the last class of the semester and she invited me to be there as well. (I realized a week later that she was still seriously ill and what she wanted was to be able to be there for one more class.) I asked her if it would be all right if I read a poem to the class that I had written two years before but now thought appropriate for her. She ordered food and that last class was like a party. She collected the students' final papers and took them with her. The poem I read was as follows:

And Mary Said Yes

God said to Mary,
Will you take my son
into your body
and share him with the world?
And Mary said yes.

And God said to me
at the Eucharist,
Will you take my son
into your body
and share him with the world?

And I said no,
there is no room.
There is so much I want to do.
No, or at least not yet.
There is no room.

Had I only known
that to take in love
would crowd out nothing good
and to share love
would only make it grow.

And then God said to me
It is not too late
to take in love
and share it with the world.
Mary said yes, will you?

Sr. Mary Daniel died within the next week. Her sister was able to get me her grade book and the final papers, on which Mary had not yet been able to record any comments or to assign grades. I read the papers and found them all to be very good save one, which was mediocre. This was from a student who Sr. Mary had told me was behind in turning in papers. He had missed two classes out of about five in the weeks I was there.

I needed to turn in grades but could find nothing in the grade book, or in the final papers, to give me a strong sense that some of them, save for one student, were deserving of an A versus an A- or a B+. So I wrote down grades of A for all of them save that one who got a C and brought the grade sheet to the registrar. I only hope Sr. Mary Daniel wasn't too upset with me for being an easy grader. The students didn't seem to mind, and I knew that they had gained a great deal from her course.

The Fallacy of Time Management

I came here in 1960 as a young professional believing I had to be very careful with my time—that much was expected and there was so little time. So I budgeted my time—so much for classes, for research, for meeting with students, for exercise, for family, and even for coffee breaks. But certainly no time for smelling the roses, and none for writing poetry, and none for enjoying a chance encounter on the street.

It didn't work. I found that when one activity intruded on time meant for another, I would be out of sync and ineffective. If a student stayed a little too long in the office, I would be resentful. And then I would feel guilty. And then nothing would get done. And I would try harder, but to no avail.

I lived in Brookline and so would walk to work, on that beautiful path around the reservoir. But I didn't see the beauty. I would be reading a book or a newspaper as I walked so as not to waste time. You might even say I was a pretext to texting. I was completely oblivious to my surroundings. Then one spring I had an epiphany. It came out of a study group in my church, where we all resolved to do something positive during Lent.

I said I would walk to work without reading and just really try to see what was around me. I didn't go cold turkey--I knew that would be too hard--so I did this for two days the first week and then three the next, and then finally every day. And I began to notice the birds and the chipmunks and the budding of the trees and the thawing of ice on the reservoir as the bleakness of winter gave way to spring. I even developed a walking mantra, which went like this:

> Every step I take, I'm I touch with the earth.
> Every breath I take I'm I touch with the air.
> Every glance I take I'm in touch with the trees
> And the sky and the universe beyond
> And God the creator of all.

I found I was getting to the office much more refreshed, and I got more done in those next few hours. So the first lesson of time management is "Take time to smell the roses." You will get so much in return. Yes, time is fixed, as measured by the clock or the calendar. But time is elastic in terms of what we might achieve with it. I can spend days on a task and get nowhere. Or I can have an hour of extraordinary productivity, when I am in that state that athletes refer to as "in the zone."

And then I discovered, quite by accident, that when I managed to be a bit more giving, it impacted my relationships with students. The conversations in the office became more relaxed as we went beyond the immediate questions to a sharing of ideas. And my classes got better as I would share my stories and even my poems. (Yes, I had gone back to poetry.) I began to see that learning is an exercise in mutual enrichment whereby in giving freely we get so much in return.

On my way to work I would walk through Cleveland Circle, where I would pass by homeless people. I would resent them, for reasons I can't quite explain, and the encounters would fill me with negative energy, with the usual negative consequences. I would walk by, with my head down or straight ahead, pretending I didn't hear the question, "Can you spare some change?", but saying nothing.

Then one day I gave a flippant answer, "No, thank you," which led to a conversation. The response was "What do you mean, No thank you?" I said, "No, but thanks for asking," and he said, "That's a stupid thing to say." We went on a bit and I got to the office filled with hostility.

He had ruined my day and I had probably ruined his.
Then I wrote down the encounter, thought about it, and
knew I had to do something.

> Can you spare some change?
> The question is so perfect.
> To say no is something less than true.
> And to stoically just walk on by,
> Is not to be the person I would like to be.

> We have some very savvy people here
> With skills developed over the centuries
> Modified a bit by corporations,
> Universities, and charities and churches
> All doing what they can to get by.

> Can you spare some change?
> I have had to give it some thought.
> Perhaps we are all beggars at the table.
> So how do I respond next time
> To my brothers of the street?

Over the next few days something remarkable began to
happen, and once again I had to write it down.

> Wearied by the negative encounters,
> resolved to try a different tack
> I left the office with a pocketful of change,
> aiming to give to the first who asked.

> And the first person I came to
> was a regular, who didn't ask
> perhaps because he recognized me
> as one who never gives.

So I walked on by,
but it was cold, and he was shivering
so I turned around
and pressed the change to his palm.

And the next night I approached another.
I said, "How's it going tonight?"
"Not so good," said he. "Will this help?"
"It sure will. I thank you kindly."

And then he called out after me
"Is that a Celtics umbrella?"
"No, I got it from some fellows in Chicago.
They use the shamrock too."

"Well, in Boston it could be a Celtics umbrella."
"You are right, it could indeed."
"Okay," said he, "you have a good night now."
"I will," I said with assurance, "and you too."

We actually had a great talk about the Celtics. And it continued with others. I developed friendships, and I found the encounters would fill me with positive energy that carried forward to everything I did.

There was a fellow named Ed, who lived in the doorway of a shuttered store. One day he was selling a pamphlet called "Athletes in the Zone." I asked him "How much? And he said "Two bucks." I said "That's a little steep, Ed. I think I'll pass." But the next night I bought one and read it and it was terrific. And on the following day I told him, "Ed, this is great, but it isn't signed. You have to sign it for me." To which he responded, "Oh, I can't sign that. I took it off the internet." Ed was trying to make a few bucks. I can respect that. Ed had been a street performer in Switzerland, and then he got hurt and came back to the U.S. He had done some writing in the past, but not recently.

He was fascinated, as was I, with this concept of being "in the zone," or of those magic moments when everything goes just right. Anyone who has played a sport knows what I mean. I told Ed that the psychologist Mihaly Csikszentmihalyi refers to this as flow. He said, "I know, but Mazlow had it first." So we talked about Mazlow. And then one day I showed him a passage from *Anna Karenina* where Levin the farmer was cutting hay and time just seemed to pass and the job was done.

This experience of flow, or optimal performance, happens in sports but it also happens in music and in art and in writing and even in the workplace. Now just imagine what we could achieve if we could learn how to bring it on. I talked about this with Ed and ventured a theory. If we could give freely of ourselves, with no thought of reward, we would be filled with positive energy and these moments would be more likely to occur. Ed thought about this and then responded, "No, it is a matter of grace. It just happens." I thought about this for a time and then said, "But maybe those moments of grace are God's way of showing approval."

Ed had started to write again, sitting there in the doorway with a spiral notebook and a pen. He told me about his great uncle George, who had written a book on astrometeorology—using the movement of the planets to predict long-term weather patterns. He could see I was skeptical, so he assured me it had been taken seriously by

NASA. He wanted to find a copy of the book, but he had lost his library card and couldn't get another because he didn't have an address. I told him I would look for it and with some searching was able to find a copy through a used book dealer. When I gave it to him he was so pleased, and of course I was pleased—I was on a high for days. Then one day Ed was gone, and I haven't seen him since. So it is with the brothers of the street.

But what about my theory that if we can manage to be giving and loving, we will have a greater chance of bringing on optimal performance? I began to look for evidence. All the major religions had said it is more blessed to give than to receive. Yeah, really? But then I came across a book which presented empirical evidence that people who develop habits of giving tend to live happier and healthier lives.[xxx]

This holds for giving of time and of goods and of money. The authors found that causation goes both ways, from happiness to giving and from giving to happiness. The correlation was not perfect, of course, but it was statistically significant. I had already discovered that in giving of my time I got back more in return in the sense that I was so much more productive with the remaining time.

Why might this be the case, that giving of what we have gets us back more in return? It seems to flow from the social relationships that develop in connection with giving, from a tendency to worry less about our own problems when we show concern for others, and from the impact of generous behavior on those areas of the brain that are associated with pleasure and feelings of contentment. The latter, the study of neurological patterns, was to me absolutely fascinating.

It is not a sure thing of course, and it appears to work best when giving becomes a habit, or something done almost instinctively with no thought of gain or loss. It may begin with small gestures which then become a part of who we are. Could it be that what I had been discovering just by chance might be true of others as well? The evidence strongly suggested that it was.

I began to suspect that giving might even leave people better off financially, through the impact it has on productivity, and I am waiting for researchers to test this proposition. I am convinced that by turning negative into positive energy I had extended my career by an extra ten years.

So the first lesson of time management is that you need to take time to smell the roses. You don't have time not to do so. And the second is that if you can give freely of yourselves, with no thought of what it might be costing you, you will get so much more in return. And a third lesson is not to spend all of your time smelling the roses. There is still work to be done.

Part 4 – Continued Growth and Stability

William Leahy takes the Reins

William P. Leahy, S.J., succeeded Fr. Monan as president in 1996. This had to be a difficult act to follow, since Monan had been regarded by many, both within Boston College and across the nation, as the outstanding college or university president of his generation.

It was my understanding that Leahy came in with a mandate to do three things, and I say this just from the impression I had at the time rather than as one who had any privileged information.

First, he was to restore relations with the Archdiocese. Second, and this is not unrelated, he was to give at least equal billing to "Catholic" as to "Jesuit" in how we describe ourselves. Third, he was to continue the movement of Boston College toward the very top ranks of national, or even international, universities.

Relations with the Diocese were still tense in 1996 but were at least outwardly cordial, as opposed to being openly hostile for a period in the mid-eighties. Leahy's task in restoring relationships became much more feasible once Cardinal Law departed for Rome in 2002, and Leahy's effectiveness in doing so played no small part in our acquiring a major parcel of land from the Diocese, that part we now call the Brighton campus, when the Diocese needed money but no longer needed the land and buildings.

Through his sponsorship of a research and teaching center called "The Church in the 21st Century," Fr. Leahy showed how Boston College could play a leading role in discussions of how the Catholic Church might best heal from the wounds of the clergy abuse scandal and then to move forward as a moral force.

And Leahy maintained the growth trajectory, which was no small achievement. While doing this, he also realized that beauty in construction is well worth the extra cost. Boston College had that with its early buildings—Gasson, Bapst, St. Mary's, Devlin, and Lyons--but had had turned to flat functionalism with Cushing, Campion, Fulton (until its reconstruction in 1993), Carney, and McElroy. Leahy built upon the reconstruction of Fulton with the completion of the magnificent Gothic structure of Stokes Hall. He appreciated the importance of beautiful surroundings in the development of the full human person.

I wasn't much involved in university committees under Leahy, but I did talk with him from time to time and I shared with him some things I had written. I told him how much I admired him for standing up to protestors who demanded he revoke an invitation to Condoleezza Rice to be our commencement speaker in 2006. At the faculty Christmas party in 2015, when he knew I was to retire the following spring, he told me that there was something he wanted from me: memoir. So here you have it, Fr. Leahy.

Advisement and the Cornerstone Program

In 1997 I was elected to the Educational Policy Committee of the College of Arts and Sciences and was made chair of the sub-committee on academic affairs. The major issue was advisement. Boston College was strong in so many ways, and getting stronger, but in student surveys we got poor marks in terms of academic advisement. The system at Boston College was pretty much the same as the one I had known as an undergraduate at DePauw some 45 years before.

Every student was assigned a faculty advisor and was required to see the advisor at least once a semester. The hope was that the faculty advisor would reach out to the advisees and develop a close relationship from which might come meaningful conversations. The reality was that faculty were busy with teaching and research and didn't get to advisement until it was time to scramble for short appointments prior to registering for the next semester's courses.

I didn't think a whole lot about it, since my own experience with my faculty advisor as an undergraduate had been a perfunctory one which I saw as a waste of time. I had talked to other faculty I had met and pretty much gotten the advice I thought was helpful. I didn't need those extra meetings with a person to whom I felt no particular connection.

Now in 1997 I had to deal with the issue. It was a weak spot and we needed to do better. Dean Robert Barth and his associate deans had begun to talk about the issue and had arranged for a speaker to come in from Marquette University to discuss what was called there a "Cornerstone" program. A faculty member would meet with a group of 12 freshmen for a series of 12 weekly meetings in a one-credit course to be graded Pass-Fail. The instructor would get to know the students and would be their advisor for at least the first year.

A program modeled on that from Marquette began to take shape. There would be a series of short readings designed to get freshmen to think about what they would like to get out of college, and there would be discussion through a process called "shared inquiry" which was supposed to get freshmen accustomed to both critical analysis and participation in discussion. The classes would end at Thanksgiving, so as to let both students and faculty prepare for final exams in other courses, but the instructor would be the students' faculty advisor for at least that entire first year.

Our sub-committee discussed the proposal, solicited feedback throughout the faculty, and got a positive response. We were prepared to bring it to a vote when we were presented with an alternative. This one was from Fr. Joseph Marchese, who was the director of the First-Year Experience. I knew Joe and respected him and so I read his proposal with some interest. It was for a three-credit course for freshmen, to be called Courage to Know. Like the one we already had on the table, it would be a small seminar with the instructor to continue to be the students' advisor. It would differ in that it would be for three credits rather than one, would be graded as any three-credit course, and would include two Boston College seniors as mentors to the freshmen.

Now we had two options. The first, the one-credit course, already had a sizeable constituency behind it, but the second had attractive features. Moreover I was led to believe that our new president, Fr. Leahy, really liked the second one. He wasn't about to dictate educational policy to us, and I did not initiate a conversation with him about the program.

Our subcommittee talked it through and decided to recommend the first for implementation in fall 1998 but with the understanding that we would likely approve the second as well if some technical details could be worked out. This took a bit of time but by fall 1999 we had the second one up and running as well.

The two were alternatives for freshmen. No one could take both, and no one had to take either one. Both proved to be popular and were oversubscribed at registration. I didn't teach one in the first few years, since I didn't care for some of the readings in the "shared inquiry" version and I was not in a position to take on an additional three-credit course as would be required for the second.

Within a few years the "shared inquiry" course was converted into "Topics" seminars in which the instructor chose his/her own readings. Now I jumped in. I called mine "Exploring Financial Markets through Reading the Wall Street Journal," and I had a ball with the course. We read the Wall Street Journal and talked through the articles that caught the interest of the students. The students had selected this seminar because they wanted to learn about financial markets, and we did this through discussion. I provided a short book that explained key financial concepts and we looked up terms as we went along.

I did not assign homework on the grounds that the students already had five other courses that required a good deal of work. The course would be graded "Pass-Fail," and the only requirement for passing was that the students come to class. The students did understand that missing more than one class without a very good reason would mean a grade of "Fail." The students came to class and they began to see it as a refuge in a turbulent first year, a place where they could talk freely about a topic that interested them and did not feel any grade pressure.

The students got to know me and I got to know them. We did an outing together in Boston or we had dinner together in my home. I shared my poetry with them and we talked about issues beyond financial markets. To me this was a major step forward in terms of advisement. We followed this a few years later with the establishment of an Advisement Center, which in my judgment was another major step forward.

Intersections and Halftime

In 2001 Boston College was awarded a significant grant from Lilly Pharmaceuticals, one which had a major impact on its continued journey of discovery. Lilly was funding programs "that help students make life choices from a faith perspective."[xxxi] Two important parts of the program were the Intersections Seminars and Halftime. The seminars brought faculty and staff together to discuss how they jointly impact the career choices that our students make and how both the Jesuit heritage and our own faith outlook may affect how we relate to students. I eagerly signed up for an early seminar, in summer 2002, and I found it both enriching and informative. I saw this as one more step by which Boston College could remain distinctively Catholic and Jesuit even as it continued to rise to the top ranks of universities.

A second key component was the Halftime program, through which students came together for a weekend away from campus at the end of sophomore year to reflect on what they had done thus far in their college careers and what they might do going forward. The locations ranged from Plymouth, Mass., to Central Vermont to Waterville Valley in New Hampshire, and in later years to the BC retreat house in Dover, Mass. Students were divided into small groups of about eight, each with a student "lead" (a BC junior or senior), and with a "sweep" (a faculty or staff member).

I was invited to be a sweep and once again was eager to go. I attended six of them over the years 2003 to 2009. Each time I chose the weekend just before fall classes were to resume, and I found myself refreshed and invigorated once classes began. I gathered from comments that the students' reaction was the same. To be together in a bucolic setting, to watch together the Michael Himes video on three key questions, and to talk about life choices in a setting where no one is being graded, was valuable, to say the least.

There were large sessions of all of us, small reflection groups, journaling, and of course games and hiking. Sweeps (faculty and staff) were asked to share in a large setting both a key passage from a favorite book and a crucial decision in their own lives.

My book passage was from *The Cathedral Within*, by Bill Shore.[xxxii] Shore pointed out that the Cathedral of Milan took hundreds of years to build, and that those who worked on it did so with the realization that they would not see its completion in their lifetimes. Yet they worked on, building something that would prove to be of immense beauty.

Shore's "Cathedral Within" was the good society as envisioned both by humanists and the major faith traditions, and it was something on which we might all be builders. Any act of love, or of kindness or generosity, is placing a brick in that cathedral, and it is worth doing even if we have no hope of seeing completion within our lifetimes.

My key decision was whether to take into our home a friend who was being released from prison after spending five years there on a fraud conviction. His wife had divorced him, his children weren't speaking to him, and he had to be in the Boston area to be able to report to his parole officer. I had been corresponding with him and as he neared release he was asking whether I might help him find a place to stay. I asked mutual friends if they could take him in but everyone had an excuse.

My wife Candy and I did have a spare bedroom, but I had serious doubts, asking myself whether I could put my family at risk, not knowing how prison might have changed someone. I did tell him he could at least have his things sent to our home, and as the packages arrived from the Federal penitentiary, the delivery people must have been suspecting that someone was coming home. I arranged for a room for him at the YMCA. But then on the Sunday

167

before he was to be released the Gospel reading in our church was the passage from Matthew, "Inasmuch as you did it for one of the least of these, you did it for me."

What were we to do? Candy and I talked it over and we took him in. In relating this to students at Halftime I emphasized that this might not have been a wise decision—the danger could have been real—but that it turned out to be good for me and my family. My son had a ball talking with our guest about prison life, my friend went on to find a place of his own after a month, and he eventually restored his relationship with his children. We are good friends to this day.

I pass these stories along to give a sense of what was happening through the Intersections program. We had a genuine sharing which in many cases gave us a renewed sense of purpose, with a faith perspective where it was meaningful to us, or barring that at least with a humanist perspective. The sharing helped me to better appreciate my own journey, and I see Intersections and Halftime as a large part of the journey of Boston College as it entered the new millennium.

September 11, 2001

I had a class at 10:30 that Tuesday morning and had come in early both to get prepared and to check on the opening of the market. I had the computer on CNN. The first story was that a plane had crashed into the World Trade Center. Then we learned that the second tower was hit and that second one went down. The Pentagon had also been hit by a plane. My wife Candy called me to ask if

I was aware of what was happening. As I left for class the South Tower was down but the North One was still standing.

I walked to class, noting how quiet it was and how the sky was its brightest blue without even the hint of a cloud. But something major had happened and we were just beginning to realize what it was. I asked the students what they had heard and we were all pretty much in a state of shock. I went on with the class and at the end learned there would be a Mass on the O'Neill plaza at noon. I went, with a host of others, and then went to my other class at 1:30. This time we began the class with a moment of silent prayer. We were all wondering whether we might have lost someone who was close to us.

In the following days the names began to come in. And I would say, "I knew that kid," or "I had that student in class." Six of my students were lost in the towers, five of them from my course in capital markets, and they were all a part of my extended family. I went to a memorial service for one of them and commiserated with his parents. No parent should have to lose a child, and in this case they didn't even have remains to put to rest.

I wondered what I could do and I needed to express myself. So I started by writing the following lines, which I shared with my classes then and over the years.

Six Students

For Patrick, Bryan, Welles, Sean, Stacey, and Brad

I lost six students on September 11,
five of them from a course in capital markets,
which sent so many to Wall Street.
They were all a part of my extended family.
They were in the towers and then they were gone.

We bowed our heads in a moment of silent prayer
and I promised my class I would try to tell their story.
People want to provide a better life for their children
and people are creative--they have ideas.
But to bring ideas to fruition, they need money.

And that's what capital markets do.
They bring together people with ideas and people with money
and they help us to be co-creators with God.
Markets aren't perfect, just as people aren't perfect,
but they are good and what these students were doing was good.

I lost six students on September 11.
They took these six and more and they took the towers,
but they cannot take the truth.
The truth survives and thus they survive
and the truth will make us whole.

And then I wrote a piece called "Markets are Good," which I shared with students, particularly those in my Capstone course called Business as a Calling.

In 2002 I was approached by a group called Trial Lawyers Care with a request to do pro bono reports on economic loss to the families of victims. I leaped at the chance and this gave me a bit of solace. A number of family members wrote touching notes of thanks, and I could only marvel at this. They had lost loved ones and all I had done was write some reports.

Boston College built a beautiful labyrinth on the north lawn outside Bapst Library, with the names of those students who were lost inscribed in stone, and I walked the labyrinth on the anniversaries of September 11. One of the five from my course in Capital Markets was Welles Crowther, the man with the red bandana. I wish that I remembered him better from class. He was a good student but did not make a notable impression at the time. On September 11 he showed extraordinary courage in leading people down from the tower and then going back for more until the tower collapsed around him.

In 2011, as a part of honoring the victims, Boston College chose as its freshman convocation speaker Colum McCann, whose most recent work was *Let the Great World Spin*. The book is about New York City and in many ways is about the events of September 11, 2001. It includes a touching chapter on how Philippe Petit had walked on a tightrope between the two towers in 1974. I had read the book in order to be able to discuss it with my Cornerstone students and was thinking about it as I walked the labyrinth. I wrote the following to describe my thoughts.

September 2011

They thought they could crush our spirit
But those acts of selfless love
Of the man with the red bandana
And all the first responders
Have trumped the violence of that day

We will always have the images
of the crumbling of the towers
As vivid now as of yesterday
But as we walk the labyrinth of our souls
And rightly mourn those taken far too soon

We begin to see another image
One of immense courage and beauty
And sheer audacity of the human spirit
Of a man dancing between the towers
On a tightrope in the sky.

And what do we see as we look upward
And see him prancing on the wire?
What flutters in the gentle breeze?
Could that be a red bandana
As he dances in the sky?

Bill Strickland Speaks at Boston College

In February 2008 I received an email from Dick Keeley as Director of Programs for the Winston Center at Boston College. Bill Strickland was coming to speak at BC and Dick was sending me a special invitation to come and to bring my Capstone class both to the lecture and to a pre-lecture "meet and greet." Strickland was a social entrepreneur from Pittsburgh who had been awarded a MacArthur "genius grant" in recognition of his success in building a better life for kids from poor families and for former welfare mothers. He had also recently written a book called *Make the Impossible Possible: One Man's Crusade to Inspire Others to Dream Bigger and Achieve the Extraordinary.*

I was intrigued but told Dick I would like to read the book and if I liked it to share it with my students. I read the book and immediately ordered copies for the students in my Capstone Class. I thought it to be easily one of the best five books of the past fifty years. My students loved it as well and I told Dick we would be delighted to come to the event. I told the students to bring their copies of the book and get Bill to sign them. He most graciously did so and the students were thrilled. It was a remarkable evening.

I was convinced Bill Strickland's book should be our freshmen book for the next fall and that Bill should be the convocation speaker. Bill believed in jazz and ceramic arts and the importance of beauty. He was very much into flow, or "swing" as he called it, and he believed that people performed much better if they were placed in beautiful surroundings. Given what we had been doing under Fr. Leahy to make Boston College a more beautiful campus, I saw Strickland as a natural for us and in fact a "no-brainer."

I got in touch with Joe Marchese, who chaired the committee to choose the freshmen book and speaker, and urged him to consider Strickland's book. Joe put me on the committee, and all of us on the committee read this book and half a dozen others. We loved the book, but an English professor on the committee pointed out that on the cover, under Strickland's name, were the words "with Vince Rause." The book was ghost written in his view, and we couldn't possibly make it our freshmen book.

I argued that the ideas and thoughts were all those of Bill Strickland and that anyone who heard him speak would recognize that. Joe Marchese loved the book as well but we couldn't get committee approval. I used Bill's book in both my Capstone and Cornerstone courses, and Joe used it as well. And he bided his time with the committee until with different membership he got committee approval for Strickland's book.

Bill Strickland was our Freshman Convocation speaker in 2013 and he hit it out of the park. We had an evening of jazz the night before, a luncheon with faculty on the day of the talk, and his talk in the evening. In introducing Bill at the faculty luncheon, I remarked that with Bill coming to speak my bucket list was complete and I could now retire. The talk, in my judgment, was the best one we have had.

Flow, Academics and Athletics

My wife Candy and I are huge sports fans, and this holds particularly with respect to the Boston College Eagles. For quite some years we have had season tickets for football, men's basketball, women's basketball, and now recently, for men's hockey. The reason it took us so long for hockey is that we hadn't played it as kids and so weren't familiar with the game. I did know something of the great Snooks Kelley, and I had come to appreciate what Jerry York did not only for hockey but for all of Boston College.

In my Capstone course we dealt with the concept of "flow," or optimal experience. I took the position that this was something that could happen to a team as well as to an individual. One of my students, a soccer player, told me that Boston College sports was very much into flow, and that we had a sports psychologist named George Mumford who was trying to make it work. Mumford had been with the Chicago Bulls when Michael Jackson led them to all those championships, and now here he was at Boston College.

At the next women's basketball game I saw Mumford sitting behind the bench. I loved women's basketball and wondered whether he might be able to get the team to a state of flow. I knew by now that when the Chicago Bull's coach Phil Jackson moved on to the Lakers he had taken Mumford with him, and I knew that the Lakers had gone on to championships. And here was George Mumford behind the bench at our games. But it was not a great season and by the next year I didn't see him there anymore. No doubt he left on his own accord, but the observation only heightened my appreciation of how difficult it is to bring this state on.

I do believe that men's hockey entered a state of flow in the Frozen Four of their championship season of 2009-2010. In regular season play they finished second in Hockey East with a 16-8-3 record, not bad but not great. Then they won the Hockey East Tournament and the Northeast Regional, with an average margin of 2 goals, to advance to the Frozen Four. They entered the Frozen Four as heavy underdogs. But then they beat Miami of Ohio 7-1 and Wisconsin 5-0 to win the national championship. The margins here were extraordinary. Something special had happened. To watch them so dominate teams with much better records was almost to enter a state of flow myself.

The most valuable player in the NCAA tournament was a BC senior named Ben Smith, and I have a story about Ben that I have shared with a good many of my students since that time. Ben was in my Capital Markets course, which met on Tuesday and Thursday at 9:00 a.m. He was there every time on time. After the team had won the Beanpot on a Monday night, Ben was there on Tuesday morning, right on time. I said to the rest of the class, "Ben played in the Beanpot last night and he is here on time. Let that be a lesson to the rest of you." Ben was a little embarrassed but that was all right.

The first class Ben missed was when the team was travelling to Detroit for the Frozen Four. They won the national championship and on the following Tuesday Ben was back, right there in his usual seat. The other students were looking at *The Heights*, which featured a full-page photo of Ben raising his stick in jubilation on scoring the opening goal of the championship game. The students put the paper away when I came in, and we went on with the class.

Thursday morning, on checking my email, I found a message from Ben from the prior afternoon. Just that day he had signed a contract with the Chicago Black Hawks and then he got a phone call telling him to get a plane to Dallas. The Rockford IceHogs were in the minor league playoffs and Ben was to be there, playing for them. He had to go, and it could be for a week or for a month. He wanted to graduate and didn't know what to do.

I emailed Ben right back, saying, "Ben, you've been there every time and on time. You have listened and you have participated in the class. That counts for a lot in my book. I can give you a grade of B on the basis of what you have done so far. Or I can give you an incomplete and you would have until August to finish the work. The grade could go up or it could go down. If I were in your shoes, I would take the B and consider the course completed."

Ben emailed back, "Professor, can we play it by ear? If we lose in the first round I will be back for the last week of classes. If I'm back I will be happy to take the final exam and complete the final project. Is that all right?"

I responded that of course it was. The Rockford IceHogs got wiped out in four straight. Ben played and he scored but it was not enough. He was back on campus and we talked. I told Ben that I knew he had a lot of work to make up and my offer still stood. He asked if he could think about it overnight. The next day he told me he wanted to finish the work. He did so and his grade was right on the borderline between two grades, clearly in the top half of the class. We all know which grade he received.

Once grades had been turned in, I asked Ben if he would stop by. I pulled out a copy of *The Heights* with the full-page photo and asked if he would sign it for me. I told him, "Not because you are a great hockey player. Maybe you are. But I want it for the story I can tell the rest of the students." He most graciously signed it and the photo is framed and on my wall.

When I tell students the story I make sure to emphasize that I would make the same offer to any student who had been there every time and on time. For one who had been goofing off it would be a different story.

I did not have a large number of athletes in my classes, perhaps in part because I had a reputation as a tough grader. It is difficult for athletes to meet the demands of travel, practice, and competition even as they handle a full course load. I am proud of Boston College for its graduation success rate among athletes, and also for its integrity in athletics. Not once, in my eleven years as chair or fifty-six as a teacher, did I sense even a bit of pressure for special treatment of an athlete.

I have wondered, as have many academics, whether going big-time in sports enhances or detracts from the academic nature of the institution. Sometimes it does seem as though football reigns and the school is attached only to give an excuse for not paying the athletes. Football is huge in our culture, as it has been for 100 years. Well before pro football, college football was "the sport" in America from the end of one baseball season to the next.

For quite some years I have polled my freshmen advisees shortly after they arrived, asking them whether the effort by Boston College to be big-time in sports was a plus or a minus in terms of their decision to come here. Over 80% said it was a plus and most of the rest said it was not a factor. The students coming in with the best records were equally adamant in saying it was a plus. I would like to see the question asked more systematically, but I clearly believe it to be a net plus.

Money is huge in college football. And with TV and live-streaming as it has developed, there is a danger of "winner take all," with the top programs scooping up most of the money and all the rest operating at a loss. The Knight Commission in 2010 made strong recommendations on revenue sharing and academic standards.[xxxiii] It is up to the presidents in the power conferences to make sure that these recommendations, or variants on them as they see fit, are implemented.

Some of my faculty colleagues resent the fact that the football coach is paid more than they themselves are, but that never bothered me. I am sure our chief fundraiser also gets a lot more than I ever did. But then I am an economist. And in terms of what we do for faculty, we have added a good many endowed chairs, which offer prestige, money, and support to academics.

Were we College Football's National Champions in 1940?

In 2015 a bit of controversy developed on campus over our claim to the national championship of college football in 1940. We assert as much in our football records and there is a large plaque at the Patriots football museum in Foxboro that says the same.

Boston College has claimed the national championship on the basis of an undefeated season that included a win over Tennessee in the Sugar Bowl. Tennessee, previously unbeaten, had rolled over its opponents in the Southeastern Conference by a combined scored of 163 to 12. But Minnesota and Stanford, likewise undefeated, also claim to be the 1940 national champions, as does Tennessee. All three of the latter base their claim on ratings by various systems, including an Associated Press poll, which were done on the basis of regular season records. None of the recognized systems, as listed in NCAA historical records,[xxxiv] had named Boston College as number one.

This led my good friend Ben Birnbaum to debunk the Boston College claim to a championship in his marvelous book written with Seth Meehan, *The Heights: An Illustrated History of Boston College, 1863-2013,* which was published in 2013.

This dismissal of our claim led another good friend and colleague Dave Twomey to point out that that there were no recognized rankings in 1940 that were done as they have been more recently, including bowl games. Had there been such rankings, Boston College would undoubtedly have finished higher than Tennessee and might very well have been number one, at least under some of the ratings systems. We have a claim to at least the "mythical" national championship, as does Minnesota, Stanford, and Tennessee.

In early 2016 Dave put together a very special evening which included a showing of film of the 1941 Sugar Bowl game and then a discussion of the season. The film was black and white and grainy but it was a record of a magnificent football game and it was great fun to see. Dave had been a student of mine in my first year of teaching at Boston College and now he was a distinguished professor in our Business Law Department. He knew I was an avid sports fan and that I would enjoy the evening. He even presented me with a jacket that says Boston College, National Champions, 1940.

So where do I come down on the issue? When I look at the huge plaque at the Patriots football museum, I feel no desire to have it taken down. And I wear the jacket with some pride.

Evolution as a Teacher

The first thirty years at Boston College were not easy for me. I was a failure in terms of published research, and my teaching was "adequate." I was not a natural in the classroom, as were a number of my colleagues who seemed to "get it" from the very first day. But I worked hard at it, and I accepted such challenges as teaching econometrics, even though I had no graduate training in the field, and teaching a large lecture class in principles of economics.

The request to teach a large lecture class came as a result of pressure to have more of our senior faculty teaching in the university core. Our course in Principles of Economics satisfied the social science core requirement as well as being the first course in our major and a required course for all students in the Carroll School. It thus had a sizeable enrollment and the only way we could have most of the students taught by senior faculty was to offer three large lecture classes with about 300 students in each of them.

We would have our "star" faculty lead the class twice a week and then have the students meet in small discussion sections to be led by our Ph.D. students. When our chair Joe Quinn asked me to teach one of our large lectures beginning in fall 1989, I suspected it was revenge for my persuading him to succeed me as chair in 1988. I was hardly a star, but my small sections by this time had grown to 55 or 60, so how different could 300 be? And my teaching had improved a bit over the years.

Teaching the class of 300 turned out to be a rewarding experience. Part of the challenge was to hold an audience and in high school I had been good at theater. I knew the material and found that I could deliver it. In the course of two semesters of principles of economics, I could talk about anything I liked. I loosened up a bit and shared much of my life story, as well as some of my poetry. The students seemed to like this and the class was oversubscribed. There were bad days of course but more good than bad. I would leave the class energized and elated. I was coming into my own.

By the early nineties I came to realize that all of my classes were fully subscribed and some of my best students were asking me to direct their senior honors theses. (This of course may have been because I had been the one to urge them to write a thesis.) This too turned out to be rewarding. For in meeting one on one for an hour or more each week, we were genuinely learning together and the students were turning out some great work.

The one-on-one work with our very best students just got better and better. Over the years 2002 to 2013 three of my students were awarded the Giffuni Prize for the best thesis in economics and a fourth was awarded distinction for his thesis in the A&S Scholar of the College Program.

Then in fall 2014 a senior named Stephen Ferguson asked me if he could do independent study with me. He wanted to work on Schumpeter and Lonergan and had been sent to me by my colleagues Fred Lawrence from our theology department and Pat Byrne from our philosophy department.

Stephen was a philosophy major with a minor in economics. Schumpeter was a giant in the field of economics who to his great dismay had been eclipsed by Keynes. At Harvard he had been the thesis advisor to my mentor in graduate school, Hy Minsky. Bernard Lonergan, S.J., was one of the most eminent theologians of our time and was a Jesuit who had tried his hand at economics in the wake of the great depression of the 1930s.

I was intrigued. I had been teaching what Minsky said on financial crises for some years and for the past three years had intensified that with a new course on the history of financial crises. I had read Lonergan's essay on macroeconomics, appreciated how he had drawn on Schumpeter, and saw insights that were close to those of Minsky. I talked to Stephen, reviewed his record, and was encouraged. I asked him to put together an outline of what we might do in the course of a semester and on receiving it was very favorably impressed.

The work with Stephen turned out to be enormously fruitful. He was a dedicated and insightful student, and through our conversations I gained a better understanding of Lonergan's work. I even came to see what I thought was an error in Lonergan's model and set out to correct it by writing a paper on it.

I had talked to Lonergan just once, and that by phone shortly after he arrived at Boston College in 1975. I had called him in my role as chair of economics to invite him to give our faculty a seminar on his essay in economics. He responded that he would be delighted to do so but that he hadn't read the literature in economics for thirty years and would need a few weeks to catch up. We ended the conversation with the understanding that we would be back in touch, but I didn't call him back and he didn't call me.

We were both busy and let it go. I wish now that I had persisted.

Lonergan had not published his essay in macroeconomics at the time of his death in 1983, and I am convinced that this was because he realized it was not as good as it could be. His followers did publish it after he died, but it drew little attention from economists. I read the manuscript only after Lonergan's death, and that was in connection with a seminar devoted to it by my colleagues Pat Byrne and Fred Lawrence.

I came to realize in 2014 and 2015 that Lonergan had important insights to offer in terms of human behavior in the realm of economics, that these were similar to what had come from Minsky, and how a greater appreciation of what they had written might have helped us to see what was happening in the years prior to the global financial crisis of 2008.

And this happened in large part because when a student approached me for independent study, I didn't just say no. I asked him to give me a detailed proposal.

So What Induced me to Finally Retire?

I never liked the term "retire," as it is commonly understood—playing golf, travelling, or sitting in an easy chair waiting to die. I prefer to think of it as re-tire, or putting on the snow tires for a new season. So why did I retire, or at least stop teaching, after 56 years at Boston College? First, I had noticed over the past few years that it was taking me more time, rather than less, to do a good job. I did think my courses were getting better each year—I was finally getting the hang of it—but to make this happen I had to be in the office on every Saturday and more often than not on Sunday afternoons.

So why was it taking more time rather than less? The memory wasn't quite the same, so I couldn't leave anything to chance. I had to have every aspect of a class there in written form, whether I had to look at the notes or not. In the old days I could go in there and wing it and it would be all right. I couldn't take that chance now.

In early spring 2014 Michael Resler called me to tell me I was to receive the Phi Beta Kappa teaching award. Michael Resler was the president of the local chapter of Phi Beta Kappa and was himself a past recipient of the award. He was highly respected as both a great teacher and a wonderful human being.

So I was dumfounded. My teaching evaluations had been all right but not spectacular. I had thought of myself as a good teacher, one who did his job, but not great.

I asked Michael how this had happened. He told me that each year the students newly admitted to Phi Beta Kappa name a professor who has had a profound impact upon them. The votes cumulate over time and in each year the professor with the most cumulative votes at that time is named the winner.

"Oh," I said, "that explains it. If you get a few votes each year, after 50 years the votes sort of add up." "No," he said, "they aren't cumulated over that length of time, and the comments given were very, very warm." So I accepted it, and I began to think that maybe I could go out on top. This was an award that was determined by a vote of the best and brightest of our students. Perhaps it had been okay to pick up my paycheck over all those years.

Getting the award did put the pressure on. I could imagine students in my class the following year turning to each other and saying, "This guy got an award?"

In that same spring, my course in Capital Markets had been featured in *Boston College Magazine* as one of those that filled up the fastest, and I knew this wasn't because I was an easy grader. I still graded pretty much as I did in the sixties, giving a grade of A to only the very top students. The recognition in *Boston College Magazine* as "most popular" also meant pressure in terms of delivering what students signed up for.

I decided to go for two more years and then stop. This would give me time to wind up my consulting practice by refusing to take new cases, as that was not something I wanted to continue in retirement. I wanted to reinvent myself, to find something new.

Moreover, 56 would be a good number. It was the length of Joe DiMaggio's hitting streak, and in my mind Joe was second only to Ted Williams. Fifty-six is the product of eight times seven. Eight is the digital root of the month and day of my birth, 7/28 (7 plus 28 equals 35 and 3 plus 5 equals 8) and seven of the year of my birth, 1933. (You can do the math on this one.) Finally, seven was the number of classes I had missed at Boston College, or one every eight years. I am not big on numerology, as you can tell, but there might be something to it.

When David Ortiz announced that 2016 would be his last year, I knew the timing was right. Big Papi and I could go out in the same year and we could go out on top. And the digital root of Big Papi's number 34 is 7 (3+4). And if we think of 2016 as oh-sixteen, then the year of our retirement has a digital root of 7. How many signs does it take to know that something is right?

My very dear friend and our department administrator, MaryEllen Doran, put together a wonderful party for me in that most meaningful of rooms, Gasson 100. The capacity of the room was just 200, so we limited the guest list to just close friends at Boston College, leaving out not only current and past students but my brother and sister as well. So, please, if you were not invited, know that I love you. Three of those Jesuits who had a major impact on my life--J. Donald Monan, James A. Woods, and Joseph Appleyard—made an appearance. I was deeply touched.

I did have a chance to say farewell to our honors students in economics through speaking at their spring banquet, and our Dean of Arts and Sciences, Greg Kalscheur, S.J., asked me to give the address to the College's Honors Award Ceremony on the day before commencement. His introductory remarks were much too kind, but he was another Jesuit whom I greatly admired. We had gotten to know each other in an extended seminar a few years before. And then the video operation of *Boston College Magazine* did a parting interview which you can find by searching "Harold Petersen Role of a Lifetime" should you have a bit of morbid curiosity.

Finally, in that last semester, I learned I had a paper accepted for publication, the one on Lonergan, Schumpeter, Keynes, Minsky, and mainstream economics. So maybe I wasn't a failure, just a late bloomer. There is always hope.

Endnotes

i Gasson Hall is the tower building, seen as the center of the campus both geographically and architecturally.

ii For information on how these towns got their names, see *Minnesota Geographic Names: Their Origin and Historical Significance,* by Warren Upham, Minnesota Historical Society, 1920 and subsequently updated.

iii *Amos and Andy* was a popular radio program in the 1940's and 1950's which later became highly controversial due to its stereotypes of life in the Afro-American community.

iv To the best of my recollection the participants in the Wall Street Program were all males. We have made some progress since then.

v John Maynard Keynes, *The General Theory of Employment, Interest and Money,* 1936. Young economists everywhere were embracing this new way of looking at how massive unemployment could persist.

vi Material in this and the following paragraph is largely taken from a portrait of Bourneuf by Paul Samuelson in *Notable American Women: A Biographical Dictionary, Completing the Twentieth Century,* Susan Ware, editor, Belknap Press, 2004. Alice Bourneuf did not often talk of herself or of her life prior to Boston College.

vii St. Mary's Hall is the Jesuit residence at Boston College, where in 1959 virtually all of the BC Jesuits lived.

viii *The Pocket Guide to Jesuit Education* is a remarkable primer on Jesuit education made available through the Intersections Program at Boston College.

ix "Prof. Daly fired, no promotion, or extension," The *Heights,* March 11, 1969, p. 1.

xi The 1957-58 number is taken from "The President's Report" in *The Heights,* December 6, 1957, p.1, and the 1967-68 number is taken from the *Boston College Fact Book, 1971.* As a caution, the numbers may not be strictly comparable.

xi The information on Phi Beta Kappa is taken from Charles F. Donovan, S.J., et al., *History of Boston College: From the Beginnings to 1990,* p. 303.

xii *The Heights,* Volume XLIX, September 24, 1968, p.1.

xiii For a wonderful account of this, see the piece by my colleague Loretta Higgins, "Coeducation but not Equal Opportunity: Women Enter Boston College," chapter 8 in a book edited by Leslie Miller-Bernal and Susan L. Poulson, *Going Coed: Women's Experiences in Formerly Men's Colleges and Universities,* 1950-2000, Vanderbilt University press, 2004.

xiv The date of this meeting and a number of other dates were checked against stories in *The Heights* as of that spring.

xv The dust bowl was the campus green, surrounded by Fulton, Carney, McGuinn, and Devlin Halls. It was the gathering place for rallies and demonstrations. As such it often became devoid of grass and thus the dust bowl.

xvi *Report of the National Advisory Commission on Civil Disorders, February 1968,* commonly referred to as the Kerner Report, after its chair, Otto Kerner.

xvii In 1975 the Black Talent Program was replaced by Minority Student Programs and in 1979 this became the AHANA Program (African American, Hispanic, Asian American, and Native American).

xviii On a prior page I referred to Fr. Donovan as the Dean of Faculties. His full title was Academic Vice President and Dean of Faculties.

xix Audited financial statements of Boston College for 1971 and *Boston College Fact Book* for 1972.

xx *Report of the National Advisory Commission on Civil Disorders*, February 1968.

xxi The text I was using and continued to use was *Economics*, by Paul A. Samuelson.

xxii Robert G. Murphy, "The Relation between a University's Football Record and the size of its Applicant Pool," *Economics of Education Review*, 1994, 13, (3), 265-270.

xxiii *The Boston College Bulletin, University General Catalog 1960-61*, December 1960, p. 13.

xxiv George Marsden, *The Soul of the American University: From Protestant Establishment to Established Disbelief*, 1994.

xxv Richard Feynman, *The Meaning of it All: Thoughts of a Citizen-Scientist*, 1998.

xxvi *Lawyers Journal*, a Publication of the Massachusetts Bar Association, December, 1994.

xxvii Following September 11 the U.S. Government established a Victim Compensation Fund and appointed attorney Kenneth Feinberg as a Special Master to determine compensation for families of victims who would accept this channel as an alternative to suits through the courts.

xxviii Connolly House is a beautiful house on Hammond Street, acquired by Boston College in 1976, which has served as a meeting place for faculty events as well as the home of Irish Studies.

xxix Michael Novak, *Business as a Calling: Work and the Examined Life*, 1996.

xxx Christian Smith and Hilary Davison, *The Paradox of Generosity*, 2014.

xxxi "Gaining direction through Intersections," *The Patriot Ledger*, October 9, 2001.

xxxii Bill Shore, *The Cathedral Within: Transforming Your Life by Giving Something Back*, 1999.

xxxiii This was the third of a series of reports by the Knight Commission on Intercollegiate Athletics. It was called *Restoring the Balance*.

xxxiv Wikipedia, citing the NCAA Football Bowl Subdivision Record Book, shows ten rating systems listing Minnesota as Number 1 in 1940, with three listing Stanford as Number 1 and two listing Tennessee as Number 1.

Index

AAUP, 43, 45
AHANA, 63, 98
Affirmative Action, 89, 91-92, 95
Alchemist, The, 149
All Saints Church (Belmont), 32
All Saints Church (Brookline), 41, 79
Alpha Sigma Nu, 115
Amos and Andy, 7
Anderson, James, 86
Anna Karenina, 157
Appleyard, S.J., Joseph, 112, 149, 187
Arnott, Richard, 124
Aronoff, Samuel, 67-68
Arrupe, S.J., Pedro, 112, 115
Astrometeorology, 157
Barth, S.J., Robert, 144, 146, 162
Baum, Christopher (Kit), 86
Bilodeau, Gerald, 68
Birdsall, S.J., William, 88
Birnbaum, Ben, 180
Bishops' Letter (on the U.S. Economy), 124-126
Black Studies, 48, 52, 62-63, 78, 82, 89
Black Talent Program, 62-67, 70, 73-74, 79, 89, 91, 94, 97-98
Bluestone, Barry, 86
Boston College Magazine, 126, 186-187
Boston Security Analysts Society, 126
Bourneuf, Alice, 3, 4, 17-31, 34, 45, 48, 75, 77, 92-93, 110
Bretton Woods, 19
Brookline, 41, 52, 79-82, 90, 94, 136-137, 153
Brown University, 14-16, 20, 36, 75-76, 118, 139
Buckley, S.J., Michael, 116
Budget Committee, 57, 82, 98-102
Business as a Calling, 146-147, 149, 170
Byrne, Patrick, 182, 184
Campanella, Francis (Frank), 83, 99, 107
Candy (Karen Dutton Petersen), 31-34, 167-168, 174
Capstone Program, 145-152, 170, 172-174
Carovillano, Robert, 71
Carter, Jimmy, 100
Cathedral Within, The, 167
Catholic, 1-2, 7, 18, 21-23, 29, 33-34, 41, 45, 109-116, 122, 124-126, 150, 160-161, 166
Cheney. S.J., Robert, 114-115
Church in the 21st Century, The, 161
Climax (town in Minnesota), 6

16100373R00115

Made in the USA
Middletown, DE
22 November 2018